IF YOU AIN'T CHEATIN', YOU AIN'T 'TRYIN'

and other lessons I learned in the Army

JOY DAMIANI

Printed in the United States.

Cover design by Joy Damiani
Book design by Asya Blue Design

ISBN 979-8-218-07307-7 Paperback
ISBN 979-8-9869754-0-5 Ebook

AUTHOR'S NOTE:

*The people, places, and events in this book
are true to my recollection of them.*

*Some names and identifying details have been changed to
protect the privacy of the individuals depicted. Dialogue has
been re-created from journals and memory.*

*These chapters are my response to a dozen years of
questions about my life as a soldier. If you've ever asked,
this is where you'll find some kind of answers.*

*Feel free to leave this book around your local military
recruitment station after reading! You'll find it's full
of valuable information that could save recruiters
a great deal of work.*

*Dedicated to every veteran who has lived
these lessons and to every young person
who learns them for the first time here.*

TABLE OF CONTENTS

The author at age 24, hoping for the best and preparing for explosions.
Baghdad, Iraq, March 2007.

JUST LIKE JOURNALISM

The ideal candidate for an Army journalism job is a high-school dropout between eighteen and twenty-five—old enough for all parts of the brain but the judgment center to be functional, and young enough to be unaware of this critical handicap. Smart enough to write journalistic propaganda, naive enough to do so without critique. My nineteen-year-old self fit the profile embarrassingly well. I knew the names of the president and vice-president, but very little about them, other than that George W. Bush said he was a Christian, and so did my family. I knew the pledge of allegiance and the national anthem, and on September 14, 2001, I vowed to Never Forget and lit a candle with the rest of the nation—at least, I lit a disposable lighter. It was the only flame to be found in my friend Meghan's '92 Toyota Sunfire. After a futile search for a candle, we'd pulled over to the side of the road and hopped out of the car at seven p.m., the appointed time for national solidarity. The Bic's flame flickered patriotically in the summer breeze.

Now here I am, sitting on my barracks bed, remembering a friend I hardly had time to know, who's just become a victim of a war I don't understand. Theoretically, I am an aspiring journalist. Technically, I am an Army public affairs specialist. I was told the job would be a stepping stone. In reality, it's more like a tightrope.

—

"We're going to have to pull your story from the front page," Sergeant Benson announced in my direction a few days ago, stomping into the back room of the Fort Stewart public affairs office where we, the understaffed print section, were scrambling to finish the last weekly post newspaper of May 2004. The creaky old floor shuddered under her boots, shaking the ancient, flimsy desks that will never be replaced, and settled with a groan as she dropped joylessly into her chair. The late-spring skies were blue, but the office stayed dark regardless of the weather outside.

"Ugh, why?" I grumbled. "It's already laid out."

"Yeah, well, we have to put a KIA on there."

"There's still plenty of room on page two ..."

The killed-in-action section might need an expansion, I mechanically considered, momentarily calculating the dead in terms of column inches. The mission in Iraq was declared accomplished exactly a year ago, but somehow, soldiers keep managing to die there.

"It has to go on page one," Sergeant Benson retorted flatly. "And we need to cover the memorial service." She sat down at her desk and threw me her trademark overworked editor look before turning back to the stack of red-ink-peppered pages the colonel just handed her, glaring at them like each one owed her money.

I sighed. "All right, all right."

"How kind of you. I'm sure Private—" She sounded out the name printed in front of her. "Tu-a-zon's family will appreciate it."

I spun around in my chair. "Private Tuazon? Is that what you said? Andrew?"

"Yeah. He was an MP." She raised an eyebrow. "Why? You know him?"

My stomach tightened. "A little." He was friends with my roommate. She was also in the military police battalion.

"Well, then maybe you should be the one to cover the memorial service. It's tomorrow." She paused before adding, "You don't have any pictures of him, do you?" Back from Baghdad less than a year, Sergeant Benson was all business. I understood—as female soldiers, the maximum range of emotion we were unofficially permitted to express was limited to none. It didn't escape me that she, like everyone else in our unit who'd just come home from invading Iraq, had returned with a much lower tolerance for feelings.

As it turned out, I did have a picture of twenty-one-year-old Private First Class Andrew Tuazon, the fresh-faced MP from Virginia. I interviewed him just six weeks ago, when his battalion was on its way to Iraq and I was assigned to cover their departure for the paper. My roommate, Private First Class Davis, showed up with a couple other friends to see him off. She was the one who introduced us a few months back, in her usual friendly way.

"This is Twat!" she'd announced with a grin as we all piled into someone's car outside the barracks. He didn't seem to take offense.

"Is that your real name, Twat?" I half-joked, squeezing into the back seat beside him. He laughed a shy, slow chuckle, shaking his head.

"Nah, they just call me that because it's shorter than my full last name."

"And more fun," Davis chimed in from the front seat. "Why would you want to be called Tuazon when you can be Twat?"

He was too busy rolling a blunt to answer. If the name bothered him, I couldn't tell. With one combat tour already under his belt by the age of 20, it would take a lot more than a juvenile nickname to get under Twat's skin. At that moment, all he cared about—all any of us cared about—was packing some stony Georgia weed into those papers and inhaling it as quickly as possible. Random drug tests scared none of us; we knew by now they were rare, and it was worth the risk to get a taste of relaxation. Besides, Davis was weeks away from getting out of the military and had nearly depleted her allotment of government-issued fucks to be given for rules.

They'd only recently moved me to these barracks and after handshakes and hellos, the first words I'd spoken to my new roommate were a response to her wondering aloud whether I'd mind if she rolled a joint in the room. I told her I didn't mind, as long as she shared, and our friendship was cemented. Six days out of seven, her twinkly blue eyes were tinted red by the time I got home in the evening. She was a walking contact high: a giggly, stoned combat veteran on the verge of becoming a civilian again. It made perfect sense that she'd ended up in the military police battalion.

Like most of Davis' friends, the one she gleefully called Twat was easygoing and good-natured. I saw him a few more times before he left for Iraq and, even when he wasn't high, he maintained a relentlessly positive attitude. The night his battalion deployed, he'd given me the quote I needed for my article: "A year is a long time, but I can't wait to leave so I can hurry up and get back." His smile was sincere and sober as he said his goodbyes to Davis and me, along with a few other friends who'd stayed up late to see the MPs off.

"Take our picture!" Davis and another friend, also named Davis, threw their arms around him. I snapped the shot—Twat's head tilted to aim an amused grin at the Davis on his right as she flashed the camera an impish smirk. We all waved as the MPs boarded their buses to the airfield. As the public affairs soldier on duty, I was authorized to follow the procession further than the rest of the family and friends could go, so as to properly document the departure. I hopped up onto the platform, taking photos as the ranks of vaguely human-shaped desert-camouflage uniforms filed through the bus doors and disappeared. As Tuazon passed in front of me, I threw the formalities of military bearing to the wind and jumped down for a final hug.

"See you when you get back, Twat. It'll be over in no time."

"I hope so," he said with a small smile, shuffling toward the last bus.

I waited till the last stragglers were gone and the parking lot was clear before bagging up my camera and dragging myself back to the barracks to write the article. It was hardly different from any other piece I'd written about any other deployment—just change the proper nouns, add a few photos and bam!—"command information" complete. Like most of us at the newspaper, I took the liberty of including the quotes and photos of my friends in my stories whenever possible, and this time had been no different. A few days after he deployed, there was Twat in the Fort Stewart newspaper, his arms around two smiling women, ready to leave so he could hurry up and get back. He had no way of knowing he'd only be in Iraq for two months before his body would be shipped back to the States in a flag-draped coffin.

"So do you have a picture of him or what?" Sergeant Benson repeated, jerking me back from the lingering vision of Tuazon's barely-legal face in the bus window, his wispy mustache curving upward in a final smile before they all rolled away. "His unit called and they need a photo for the memorial service."

I nodded slowly. "It's not very good, though. His hat's covering one eye. Doesn't his family have anything?"

"Apparently not. Just his Basic Training picture. Nothing recent."

I released another sigh. "Guess it'll have to do."

"Yup. We'll run it again with your memorial story, too." She turned back to her work, then paused with a side-eyed glance in my direction. "Sorry about your friend."

———

On my barracks bed, my mind wanders to the 2000 presidential election—four years feels like a lifetime ago. I was in reform school. My only exposure to the candidates was through the debates, which we were allowed to watch with staff supervision. Little information was given to us students about the fall-out of the election (we were told there was a miscount, and eventually, that Bush was declared the winner), but even if more news had gotten through, I was too preoccupied with my own miserable circumstances to care.

I remember the day my English teacher told me he wanted me in his journalism class. It was my second day at the school. I was still coming to grips with the shock of being sent away from home at all, let alone for the purpose of being reformed.

"You're a great writer," he declared, handing back my assignment. "I want you writing for me." He was the first staff member to speak to me with anything resembling dignity.

The articles I wrote for him covered a minuscule range, from student life to sports—he knew better than to assign hard-hitting, investigative pieces to students at a school whose primary function was to torture teenagers until they stopped questioning authority. The newspapers we printed were sent to our parents, costs covered by the school's exorbitant tuition and fees. Every story we produced was carefully selected to make our parents feel good about having turned over their Troubled Teens™to a staff full of self-taught disciplinarians and teachers carrying questionable certification. My English teacher, I discovered later, had never even finished his bachelor's degree. Not unlike my military editor.

Nearly four years later, I'm still writing what I'm told and calling it news.

Back then, I knew that if I wanted to study journalism, I'd have to do it on my own. So three months after leaving reform school, I signed up for community college. Three weeks after that, hijackers flew airplanes into the twin towers of the World Trade Center. Another three months after that, Sergeant Brown called.

It hadn't taken much trying for him to convince me that my best shot at being trained as a journalist was *not* to work my way through community college and then transfer to a four-year school followed by multiple internships with an eventual small-town newspaper employment opportunity, but instead to join the military and become a public affairs specialist. It was just like journalism, he said. Maybe a little different.

———

At the memorial service, I see my photo of Tuazon everywhere—in the program, next to the door, and as a prominent poster in the front of the chapel alongside his boots, rifle, helmet, and dog tags, displayed in the traditional arrangement for a fallen soldier. It's the only recent photo anyone has of him. Davis and Davis have been cropped out, so the smile on his face is directed to an empty space somewhere off to his right, the desert-camouflage boonie cap on his head concealing his left eye. Only the two Davises and I know who'd been on either side of him: the last ones to hug their friend before sending him off to war.

I do my best to be what they call a "professional soldier"— refusing to cry as I stand in the back with my notepad and camera, listening and taking notes as my friend's rear-detachment commander explains he died honorably, carrying out the mission he'd been given. I watch my pen write the words *killed, sniper, Mosul Iraq May 10 04* in shorthand without consciously comprehending their meaning. True to his word, Tuazon hurried up and returned home—and true to mine, I am here when he gets back.

Every soldier knows not everyone comes home from war. I'm not new anymore and I know it well. The article I write about the memorial service for my friend, the first casualty whose name really means something to me, is no different from any other article I've written about any other memorial service—just change the proper nouns, add the only photo anyone has, and bam!—tribute paid. Another life, wrapped neatly in all the right words: honor, sacrifice, mission complete. Details documented: who, what, where, when, how—all except the one question we can never answer, the one we aren't allowed to ask: *Why?* I don't have time for *why*. It just keeps me from getting my work done.

Wrapped up in the technicalities of my job, its purpose ceases to matter. Along with all the memorial services, I cover deployments, homecomings, training exercises, a smorgasbord of ceremonies, sporting events, and, unavoidably, base-wide baby showers, regularly occurring a few months after the homecoming ceremonies.

Meshed with reporting and photography is the weekly grind of newspaper layout, a task that reduces most of my brain to a puddle of exasperated goo. I have no inclination to think critically of the work my fellow soldiers and I are doing, but then, to do so would require far more time and energy than I have at my disposal. Unless I allow it to cut into my drinking time—or, as I think of those precious few hours, my only open escape hatch.

———

I drop the memorial article on Sergeant Benson's desk and make my way back to the barracks, where I crack the seal on a bottle of Jim Beam. Four fingers over ice, plus a splash of Cherry Coke to mask the sting of cheap bourbon on my tongue. Davis is out of the military now and I haven't been issued a new roommate yet, so I'll have to toast Tuazon alone in our—my—half-empty room.

My nervous system is no longer shocked by another soldier's death, I realize as I watch the ice cubes swirl around my cheaply-constructed cocktail, cracking and popping their indignation at being dropped into a warm cup of spiked, carbonated corn syrup. Before hearing the soldier killed in action was a friend, my reaction to his death was the same as it was for all the others—an artisan blend of "That's too bad" and, "Does this need to affect me?"

A wave of nausea washes over my body as my mind's eye scrolls through every set of dog tags I've photographed dangling from a rifle over a set of empty combat boots, feeling nothing but annoyance at having to attend yet another memorial service and interview another grieving mother, husband, wife, another nervous rear-detachment commander carefully choosing his words. I was so proud of my well-rehearsed presentation—showing no sorrow, always professional!—but now I seem to be playing the part without trying. I didn't notice when the rehearsal ended and my live performance began. These days I recite the script without prompting.

Who wore these empty boots? Soldiers. What happened? They gave the ultimate sacrifice. Where? In the combat theater of operations. When? Every day. How? Performing their mission.

"Just like journalism," I mutter to the dark room.

The details of Tuazon's death, the ones I hastily jotted down at his memorial service before driving directly to the liquor store, still cycle through my mind on a loop. I raise my plastic cup and will the words to stop. As the whiskey hits my lips, an abandoned *Why?* floats into the rotation. *Why?* Because ... because ...

The answer is stuck in my throat. I wash it down with whiskey. After one bittersweet swallow, it dissolves. Just like it's supposed to.

IF YOU AIN'T CHEATIN'

It's the middle of a sticky summer in Fort Jackson, South Carolina, and I'm eight weeks into Basic Combat Training— far enough to know that, although I am technically capable of being a soldier, neither I nor my drill sergeants believe I ought to actually be one. I am far too entertained by the Army's attempts to indoctrinate me, I am constantly injured, and, if we're all being honest, I am probably a liability.

But the nation is at war and the Army needs soldiers. The World Trade Center towers were still spewing ash all over Manhattan when I signed on the dotted line along with every other hastily-recruited enlistee in the newly-christened Global War on Terror. I'm nineteen—energetic, broke, and smart enough to follow orders, but also, as I'm quickly discovering, dumb enough to ask none of the right questions.

———

Six months ago, the phone call came. It was one of upstate New York's classic subzero December mornings. I was getting ready to head out the door for community college. My bedroom, the one where I slept all but a few years since birth, once had walls covered in posters—swirly psychedelic art and Beatles posters brightly juxtaposed with those of No Doubt, Rage Against the Machine, 2Pac, and any other artist my parents hated—which gazed fiercely down on me throughout my adolescence. Sometime during the year and a half that passed between the day I was sent to reform school and the day I'd unceremoniously left it, my posters had come down. In their place were inspirational prints. Some included Bible verses. Every night I'd lie in bed, platitudes looming over me in the dark as I lulled myself to sleep with dreams of moving into my own place. As "I CAN DO ALL THINGS THROUGH CHRIST WHO STRENGTHENS ME" stared down from its victoriously floral frame, I couldn't help but assume that if my parents really meant for Christ to give me the strength to do *all* things, their reaction would've been entirely different when I'd worked up the strength to flee a school that made the military look like an easier option.

Propping the cordless phone on my shoulder as I answered it, I carefully applied a last swipe of mascara. A baritone voice introduced itself as Sergeant Brown with the U.S. Army. Did I have a moment to chat?

"Well I'm getting ready to go to class, so not re—"

"Oh, what are you studying?"

"Right now I'm just taking some gen-ed courses, but I'm going to study journalism after that."

"Oh yeah? You know, I could get you a journalism job in the Army right now, if you want. You'd start at $26,000 a year, and you'd even get money for college on top of it."

Maybelline wand still in hand, I paused my preparation process. The corner of my eye caught the federal financial aid application on my bed, under the *People* magazine memorializing George Harrison. Money for college, did he say? A real journalism job? My current place of employment was a kiosk in the mall stocked with designer knock-off sunglasses and cell-phone accessories. The job was simple: sell plastic crap, the more the better. The work was mind-grating, especially over the holidays when it was soundtracked with the same twenty-five consumer-tested songs piping through the mall speakers, but this had been the only option available after I'd hitchhiked the hundred-twenty miles home from reform school six months earlier. Since the day I was hired, I'd been looking for a chance to quit. *Any* chance.

Sergeant Brown finished making his offer, and it sunk in like a brick. The Army. The last time a recruiter approached me, I'd guffawed in her face. That was before I'd been sent off to have my rebellious streak wiped clean at the Family Foundation School, where tactics like public shaming, mindless manual labor, and sitting in a corner in forced silence were standard forms of discipline for crimes as benign as an untucked shirt. If the military wanted to break me down, I thought, when pointlessly picking up rocks from a soccer field for eight hours a day couldn't, it would have to use a tactic more sophisticated than pushups.

After more than a year and a half at the school, I had expected to graduate with my class. Instead, I was faced with the prospect of six more months of supervised rock-picking. I had no more major sins to hone in on, so the staff and students decided it was time to cure me of sarcasm, using their time-honored traditions of manual labor and social shunning. They pulled me out of classes, put me to work, and, when my brain stubbornly refused to relinquish its favorite coping mechanism, they left me there long enough to cancel all my plans for a June graduation.

Unable to interact with anyone, I had conversations with myself. *This is insane, right? Like, it's actually madness? This can't possibly be good for me. I could have stuck it out till June, but not another six months.* The next graduation wasn't until December, and I doubted I'd be cured of sarcasm by then, either. *When will this end? Is earning my parents' approval really worth being tortured?*

After three weeks, I worked up the courage to flee. There was no guaranteed future for me anywhere, but it was worth the risk to escape with my sanity.

My own family was unimpressed.

"Mom and Dad are changing the locks. You'd better leave," my younger brother had monotoned in my direction, without looking up from his book, upon my sweaty homecoming, the culmination of a desperate day making my way back to Syracuse through rural upstate New York. I was penniless, disgraced, and a mental mess. I didn't even have an ID, much less a driver's license. I'd taken a seat at the kitchen table anyway, and when my parents returned, I made my appeal to stay.

When they said I could stay *"if ..."* I was nodding before they'd even finished listing their conditions. Paying rent, agreeing to a ten p.m. curfew, allowing them to dictate which friends I could see, attending their church, getting as many jobs as they wanted me to have, doing whatever they wanted—it all seemed like a better option than having nowhere to go. My friends hadn't heard from me in a year and a half—an eternity, in teenage time. My parents had gotten rid of my address book, and all the phone numbers I'd memorized had been replaced by reform school regulations.

The military couldn't possibly be worse than this existence, I was sure of it. And didn't he say I'd get money for college? I was definitely going to need that money. The GED I'd managed to achieve after my first time dropping out of high school could only get me into college, not pay for it. My parents said they'd reimburse me for community college classes, but I had to front the registration fees, and no matter how long I worked at minimum wage, my hourly pay wasn't quite keeping up with my credit hours.

The six stress-filled months since I'd fled reform school flashed before my eyes in the twelve seconds it took me to give Sergeant Brown his answer. My brain was still reconfiguring itself after a year and a half at the Family School, but I was clear as a bell on one thing—even working two part-time jobs, it would be years before I could afford to study journalism.

The job Sergeant Brown had offered was alternately titled "public affairs specialist," and that was the job I'd accepted after carefully considering, for those twelve entire seconds, the alternative of continuing to live in my childhood bedroom, working at the mall for not much more than minimum wage, and coming home to the authoritarian rule of my unsympathetic parents. Joining the Army seemed to be not only the sensible option, but the respectable one, and it had the added bonus of being chock-full of potential adventures in something resembling the career of my choice.

"You'll need to sign up for five years to get the journalism job," Sergeant Brown had said with a hint of hesitation in his voice. He had no way of knowing about either the highly-restrictive environment I'd recently fled or the one I was currently attempting to flee. His initial proposal had hit my eardrums and bounced around my mind for far less time than he was expecting before I gave my answer: "Okay."

There was a moment of silence. He ventured, "So ... you know that means you'll have to ... join the Army."

"Yep, okay." Another pause. He couldn't see me fantasizing about the moment I'd finally be able to inform my parents their rules no longer applied, and tell my kiosk boss specifically where he could stick his stacks of surplus sunglasses and cell phone accessories.

"All right, well … great! Um, can I ask you a few questions first?"

"Sure." I was back to applying mascara, trying not to impale my eye while silently chuckling at Sergeant Brown's eagerness.

The recruiter cleared his throat, took an audible breath, and asked, "Are you a convicted felon?" I could almost hear him crossing his fingers.

"Nope."

"Great! Let's see, you're out of high school … do you have a driver's license?"

"No. I just had my first driving lesson."

Sergeant Brown was unshaken. "It's okay," he said reassuringly. "As long as you get it before you go to Basic. Now, let's see, do you have any health problems?"

"I have some asthma," I admitted. It rarely acted up, possibly because it was medically designated as "exercise-induced," and I never exercised if I had the option to avoid it. That option, I realized, was about to disappear.

He paused. "Hm. That's not good."

"Oh. Well, sorry, we tri—"

"Wait," he interrupted. "Ah, I don't know if I heard you the first time. Let me ask you again. Do you have any health problems?"

"Um … nope."

"Outstanding! Now, when can we schedule a meeting?"

We scheduled the meeting for the following day. I told my mom about it on my way out the door for class. From her reaction, I might have said I was taking a job getting smacked in the face with a shovel.

"Y-you? Want to join the … Army?" I could tell she was either shocked or convinced she was hallucinating—or maybe convinced I was the one hallucinating.

"Yes! They're going to give me a journalism job. Off to class now, byyyee!" I chirped, closing the door behind me as she, for all I knew, fainted.

I strode out into the biting December morning with a burst of unfamiliar pre-coffee energy. This would be one of the biggest steps I'd ever taken toward Responsibility and Adulthood and—dare I even think it?—making something of my life. I assured myself that if I didn't get what I wanted out of the military, it would only be a few years till I could get out and move onto the next thing. College money! Journalism job! Adventure! This couldn't be anything but the right decision.

After an hour in a grey government office in a beige cubicle with an ancient computer monitor, I got the required aptitude test out of the way. It felt like a slightly-simpler GED exam, but with mechanical-engineering questions. I met with Sergeant Brown to get weighed and discuss the next steps toward getting me into a uniform. He was thrilled that I could meet the aptitude standard necessary for my desired military occupational specialty, but …

"But what?" I asked with the tiniest hint of anxiety.

"Well … you're, um," he hesitated. "You're going to need to lose some weight." He averted his eyes before tentatively meeting my troubled gaze. "Just ten or eleven pounds, though. Or thirteen." Avert.

I let out a sigh, recalling how only two years earlier, my scale had read a fashionable 122. Then I was shipped off to be reformed not only psychologically, but physically, thanks to the Family School's strict rule that every student had to clean their plate at every meal. For once in my life, I'd been an overachiever, gaining thirty pounds in the first six months. After only half a year back home, my waistline had failed to reset itself, and the stretch marks on my thighs showed no signs of fading. As the first wave of depression swelled, Sergeant Brown perked up.

"Hey now," he smiled reassuringly, "you've got plenty of time. You don't need to pass the physical till next month. And if you can pass the tape test, you don't even need to lose much at all. Just get down to 133 and you'll be fine. Think you can do that by January?"

"You want me to lose weight over Christmas?" I gaped at him. "My family's Italian-American. We've been preparing for this eating season since September. What am I supposed to tell my grandma?"

"Uh, tell her you're trying to join the Army? Look, if it helps, I believe you can do it. I'll even go to the gym with you. Besides, if you really have trouble losing the weight, I know a few tricks. You'll be fine."

Already registered for spring semester at community college, I opted to enlist under the delayed-entry program and buy myself a few extra months to get into some shape other than the roundish one I was wearing. If I didn't meet the standard, I wouldn't even qualify for delayed entry. No delayed-entry, no Army, no journalism job, no college money, no escape to the rest of my life.

I started giving myself pep talks. *Come on, Self, don't you want to get back to a healthy weight? Put down the cookie. That one, too.* Having a deadline meant I might just be able to make the jump from wanting to lose weight to actually doing it. I immediately put myself on a diet and began what I considered to be a regular exercise routine: aggressive stretching, plus a light jog. This would definitely work.

———

The night before I had to report to the local Military Entrance Processing Station for my physical, I had lost a grand total of six pounds. Sergeant Baker, the wiry new recruiter with tired eyes who was taking over for the recently-reassigned Sergeant Brown, dropped me off at a local hotel, where the other potential recruits and I were instructed, formally, to get plenty of rest in preparation for the day-long evaluation process. In the morning we'd be picked up at zero-six-hundred to head over to MEPS.

Logistics established, he pulled me aside. "Okay, you just got your formal instructions. Now here's your informal instructions." He paused and looked around. I waited. "You still have to lose, what, seven pounds?"

I nodded.

He lowered his voice. "Okay. There's a gym, a sauna, and a steam room in this hotel." He was smiling, but not with his voice. He raised a ruddy hand and pointed one stern finger at me. "From this minute forward, do not eat. Do not drink water. Do not drink anything."

"Okay …"

"First, go to the gym and run on the treadmill as long as you can. Then go to the steam room as long as you can. Then the sauna. Then back to the treadmill. Repeat this rotation until you've lost seven pounds. Keep it up all night if you have to. You have to pass weight or you'll be sent home. Do you want to be sent home?" I shook my head. "Okay then. It's eighteen-hundred now, that's six p.m. I'll see you in twelve hours. Be ready on time. Remember, do not eat or drink *anything*."

A few minutes later I headed to the treadmill for my first rotation. As my door clicked shut, another recruit emerged from the next room.

"Hey!" She greeted me with a grin. "Some of us are gonna go get pizza. Wanna join?"

"Ugh, I can't." I frowned. "I have to lose seven pounds tonight."

"Oh, yeah, I have to lose five," she grinned. "But my recruiter gave me this stuff to help me out." She dug around in her purse and pulled out a green-glassed bottle. "Laxatives. He told me to drink the whole thing and stay close to the bathroom. If you want some, I'm sure I don't need it all. I'm surprised your recruiter didn't give you any."

"No, he just told me to go to the gym and then sweat the rest off in the steam room and sauna."

"What? That's bullshit. How about this—after I get back from pizza, let's go to the store down the road and get you a bottle of your own. You'll probably lose a pound walking there and back. Then we can come back here and flush the rest of the weight down the crapper."

Smiling beatifically as she casually proposed a fun-filled night of shitting our way into the Armed Forces, my new friend introduced herself as Gabrielle ("Gabby, though"). She was 17, from Elmira, and hoping to use the Army as a way to no longer be in Elmira. She didn't look overweight, but she was an entire inch shorter than my five-foot-three, which meant she had to get down to 129 pounds by morning. Along with the laxatives, her recruiter had given her specific advice about how to maneuver her way through the Body Mass Index test that awaited those of us who were holding onto extra pounds.

"What you want to do," she told me as we walked to the drugstore, "is make yourself as tall as possible. Flex your neck a bunch so that it sticks out when they put the measuring tape around it. Same with your wrists. And work on sucking in your hips. Those are the three places they'll measure."

"Suck in my hips?" I'd read hundreds of issues of *Cosmopolitan*, and nowhere in its glossy pictorial tribute to anorexia had I ever seen a step-by-step tutorial on hip-sucking—this, I assumed, meant it couldn't be done.

"Well, it's really more like sucking in the side of your butt." That sounded more feasible. "But you can't let them see you do it. If they see you sucking in they'll disqualify you. And they measure three times, so you have to make sure you suck in the same amount every time. They do this all day, so they're always watching for clenched butt muscles."

"Your recruiter told you all this?"

"Yeah, he really wants to meet his quota," she grinned again, clearly amused by the worry that had engulfed my face. "Don't worry! You'll be fine. The Army needs people right now. I have a bunch of friends already on their way to Afghanistan. They'll take pretty much anyone they can."

She had a point: it had only been four months since terrorists—who, I had noticed, weren't from Afghanistan—had flown hijacked planes into the World Trade Center and the Pentagon, and military recruitment had reached a fever pitch. There wasn't a single commercial break that missed the opportunity to tell us wide-eyed youth all about the heroic deeds (and college money!) that awaited *true patriots* who were brave enough to join what they were then calling the "Army of One." "Be all you can be," Sergeant Baker had told me, was no longer enticing enough members of the self-esteem generation. Apparently, because most of us eligible recruits were under the impression that being as much as we already were would get us through life just fine, the decision had been made to appeal to our freshly-instilled sense of rugged individualism. The Marine Corps was still being comparatively choosy, but the Army wasn't turning away any warm bodies unless they were visibly disfigured. Even then, Sergeant Baker said, there was always the possibility of a waiver.

While we walked to the pharmacy, Gabby and I discussed at length the various ways to pass a physical without having to go to the trouble of passing it legitimately. By the time we got back to the hotel, we'd concluded laxatives and visual trickery were our best options by far. Gabby had done extensive research into this process. This should have given me, as the one of us hoping to pursue a career in journalism, a small degree of embarrassment, but my mind was entirely consumed by the need to lose seven pounds, urgently.

Before retiring to our respective restrooms, Gabby and I clinked the laxative bottles together in a toast to the new, slimmer selves we were bound to be by morning.

"You know, I still might go hit the treadmill-sauna-steam room for a couple rounds first."

She shrugged. "Suit yourself. If you need me, I'll be in my room watching cartoons and dropping pounds. See you in the morning!"

—

The next day, I was starving and dehydrated. Sergeant Baker arrived at six a.m. as promised, narrowing his eyes to inquire how many pounds I'd managed to lose. When I reported that all but one had been successfully evicted, he was visibly impressed.

"Really?" He blinked. "I mean—wow! Six pounds? That's great! Just from the treadmill and sauna?"

"Well, and this ..." I showed him the empty bottle, and his eyes widened before relaxing into a look bordering on respect.

"Niiice! That is outstanding. Now, let's get you down to MEPS. Whatever you do, don't pass out."

I managed to remain conscious throughout the physical, although there were a few moments of delirium that set in while our group filled out a questionnaire in a grey-walled classroom with the recruiters waiting outside. Sergeant Baker briefed me in the hall.

"Any questions about drugs or alcohol, check *No*," he advised. "Same with any family history of medical issues. And remember— you don't have asthma. Of any kind."

"Got it!" I lilted as he steadied me. "No drugs. No alcohol. No asthma. Anything else?"

"Just make sure you sign everything they tell you to sign. Oh, and suck in your hips. Don't eat or drink anything till they've weighed you. You'll be fine. See you on the other side." He disappeared down the hall with a final thumbs-up.

By the end of the day, I was ready to collapse. Correction: I was ready to eat an enormous meal, drink a gallon of water, and then collapse. The whole ordeal was over. All I had to do now was wait for the call saying I'd passed the physical. I knew I'd made weight, and the rest of the exam was tedious but challenge-free. Exhaling the day's stresses, I finally passed out.

—

Sergeant Baker's under-enthused phone call worried me.

"Well, you passed weight and the tape test ... but there's one problem."

"Oh?"

"It's your eyes."

"What about them?"

"Um … they're bad." I chuckled.

"I could've told you that. I've worn glasses or contacts since I was five."

"No, I mean, they're really bad."

"Yeah, I know." I was getting impatient. "That's why I wear contacts. To correct the astigmatism."

Sergeant Baker cleared his throat. "I don't think you're getting me, here. The doc said you're practically blind."

I groaned and sat down, exercising every ounce of restraint at my disposal to resist making a sarcastic remark about foresight clearly not being a qualification for military service. After all the dieting, the exercise, the laxatives—the fucking laxatives!—it was for nothing, because of my stupid eyes. "Well, I guess that's it then."

"Now, wait a minute before you go giving up on me," Sergeant Baker insisted. "We might be able to get you a waiver. I already put in the request."

"But you said–"

"Yeah, I know. I don't want you to get your hopes up too high, but there's still a chance." He paused. "I won't find out for a day or two, though."

"Why would the Army want me if I'm practically blind?"

"Oh, they want you. Trust me. We just have to make sure they know you're not going to try to claim they made you blind. I'm pretty sure the waiver will come through without a problem." I could hear him shifting in his chair.

"Well, if you think so …" I hesitated.

"I'm ninety-nine percent positive the waiver will come through," he insisted. "Give it a couple of days. Trust me," he repeated. "You're going to make a fine soldier."

———

I arrived at Fort Jackson for Basic Combat Training in the dead of a humid June night, stuffed into a bus with a gaggle of other new recruits. We were herded half-asleep into one briefing after another, each one requiring a new set of paperwork and a new set of commands, all delivered in the same life-or-death tone. This was clearly meant to intimidate us brand-new baby soldiers. It seemed to work on some, but glancing surreptitiously around the crowded room at my fellow privates' faces, it was easy to see not everyone could take such contrived aggression seriously. We don't need to be frightened into filling out forms and getting blood drawn. This, I suspected, was just preparatory yelling, intended to get us accustomed to being regularly berated over the next nine and a half weeks.

But the most frightening threats, I'd already learned, are rarely yelled. When my parents saw me off at the airport, they hadn't raised their voices. My father had given me a hug. He'd said softly—affectionately, even—with a smile, "You know, if you don't finish Basic Training, you're not coming home."

I'd smiled back. These drill sergeants had a lot to learn about intimidation.

———

For the first week, the biggest challenge at Basic Training is staying awake, at all costs. A drill sergeant's yelling is nothing to take personally until it's emphatically directed at your face.

"WAKE UP, PRIVATE," comes the boom above you, sixteen seconds after your eyelids lose their grip, two hours into a three-hour class on personal hygiene. "MY ARMY'S NOT PAYING YOU

TO TAKE A NAP."

"Roger, Drill Sergeant!"

"DO PUSH-UPS TILL I GET TIRED."

The powers-that-be figured out long ago that exhaustion and compliance go hand-in-hand. A person's brain needs to be mostly awake in order to think for itself, so our mornings begin before dawn. The sentiment this fosters among recruits is almost exactly the opposite of goodwill. Each day, by mid-morning at the latest, everyone is at least moderately annoyed with everyone else. After all, we're still in the initial processing phase. None of us are guaranteed to see any of the others after companies and battalions are assigned. Any sense of camaraderie that develops, as far as I can tell, is inspired by our collective, passionate desire to get the fuck out of here as soon as humanly possible.

—

Each briefing is more tedious than the one before, but it isn't until the eye exams that the tedium is compounded by humiliation. This is the day those of us with poor vision will all remember in high-definition clarity—the day we meet our BCGs.

"Birth-control glasses" are as appropriately-nicknamed as Carrot Top, except the comedian can boast exponentially more visual appeal than the unfortunate wearer of BCGs. Each pair is carefully crafted in what I have to assume is one of the hottest fires of hell: the most durable brown plastic frames available hammered into the most universally-unflattering squarish shape. Even without the Coke-bottle lenses the most wretched of us are destined to need, BCGs transform our faces into objects of intrigue. They have the double-edged effect of applying a thick layer of shame to wearers while also handily removing our peripheral vision. It takes minimal field research to confirm that there are few less-convenient times to lose the ability to give a fierce side-eye than while wearing BCGs in Basic Training—especially if, as in my case, you happen to be as clumsy as you are blind.

"Can you see the FUTURE in those?" snarks Private Small, my bunkmate/battle buddy, as we march to the chow hall.

Small is a six-foot-tall, pale-white redhead who makes such an easy target that the drill sergeants leave her largely alone. If even *she* has jokes, I can tell that the BCGs completely cancel out any hint of toughness our newly-issued camouflage fatigues might've added to my short, squat build. I have to turn my head to make eye contact with Small.

"Only the part of the future where I'm going to trip you when you get down off the bunk in the morning." Neither of us can tell if I'm kidding.

"Better not be with your busted foot or it'll hurt you more than it hurts me."

None of my injuries heal before the next one is incurred. It isn't as though I wake up every morning and fall out of bed (although if I hadn't been assigned the bottom bunk, who knows how many more scars I'd have). It's more like, for these nine weeks, Murphy's Law, decreeing that anything which can go wrong, will, applies specifically to me. I know the whole point of Basic is to toughen me up, and I have no desire to single myself out as the soldier who can't handle pain—so as if to test my resolve, any time the opportunity to hurt myself arises, my body masochistically embraces it, blatantly ignoring my survival instinct's frantic protests. The busted foot Small refers to sits throbbing in its combat-boot cage, knowing she is right, dreading the day it will have to march again.

The first round of drill-and-ceremony training featured several daily hours of marching up and down the length of a sweltering parking lot in rectangular formation. By the end of the first day

I was entirely unsurprised to acquire an ambitious blister on top of my foot, right under the one part of my brand-new boots that couldn't be loosened. Dutifully applying moleskin and ointment each day, I didn't mention it to my drill sergeant until the blister became a gaping hole and my initially-stealthy limp resembled a pirate swagger. Multiple visits to the medical clinic yielded antiseptic, soaking salts, and an impressive pile of moleskin pads, along with the obligatory 800-milligram Motrin tablets—the Army's answer to every ailment from stubbed toe to amputation—but no noticeable reduction of the blister. In four weeks, the monstrosity had grown large enough to have its own personality. Begrudgingly accepting its refusal to leave, I'd given in and named it George. Small's moral support consisted of helpfully describing George's disgustingness during the nightly cleaning ritual, as I silently counted down the days until I never had to see her again.

———

In the fourth week of training, my other foot was taken out of commission. The task at hand was the obstacle course—officially called the Confidence Course due to the requirement not to pass, but simply attempt, each obstacle, according to the drill sergeants' grumbled orientation speeches. Despite George being a fully-grown blister beast, I managed to complete most of the elements of the course with sufficient confidence. The only one that gave me trouble was the parallel bars, which I hadn't encountered since I was young enough to call them monkey bars and easily carry my entire body weight with my arms.

Having navigated my share of monkey bars as a child, I expected them to be a cinch, especially compared to other obstacles, most of which involved climbing up and/or over ropes, nets, and walls in a hurry. Approaching the bars with what I felt certain was miles beyond the required degree of confidence, I jumped up and grabbed the first one. A moment later, my plan to nimbly swing across the bars dissolved as I found myself plummeting nimbly to the ground eight feet below, landing with confusion in the waiting arms of the spotter, a lanky U.S. Virgin-Islander named Norton.

"How—what just happened there, Norton?" I asked in a daze.

"Um ... you fell down?" Norton, even in those early days, was not known for his razor-sharp wit, although I still suspect that's just his tactic for keeping expectations low. He earned a reputation for being one of the dimmer bulbs in our company's box during the first week of training when, with an entirely straight face, he'd asked one of the drill sergeants about the proper way to fold his G-string. He was assigned the job of spotter on the parallel bars primarily because he was tall and the drill sergeants seemed to believe this was one task he couldn't possibly fail. I was not as convinced.

My second attempt to master the monkey bars went along the same lines as the first—jump, grab, fall speedily onto Norton. That time, though, I realized what had gone wrong: the parallel bars were not secure. Instead, they swiveled when grabbed. The trick was to move fast enough that no hand stayed on the bars long enough to be swiveled off. With this new information, I felt prepared for one more try.

I jumped. I grabbed. I swung ... not quite fast enough. I fell. This time though, instead of landing neatly on Norton, I hit the ground and landed squarely on my left ankle. Once again dazed, but now with the special feature of pain shooting up my leg, I managed to fix a glare in the direction of my spotter.

"What. Happened. Norton," I demanded through clenched teeth.

A drill sergeant rushed over when she saw me on the ground. "God—bless America. Norton, what in the—" she checked herself. "What happened here?"

"Drill Sergeant, I didn't think I was allowed to catch the females," he proclaimed with frightening sincerity.

She stared at him. He stared back. She stared harder, and even through blinding pain I could still see her mentally subtracting the minutes remaining in this wretched drill sergeant assignment. "God bless America," she finally muttered before turning to watch me hobble away from the bars. "Is that ankle broken, Private?"

"Probably just a sprain, Drill Sergeant," I offered in as stoic a tone as I could manage. "I'm … fine."

She rolled her eyes. "Sure you are. Go get some X-rays. And Norton!"

"Yes, Drill Sergeant!"

She stared at him. He stared back. We all knew further words were pointless. "God bless America," she grunted and stalked away.

The X-rays revealed it was indeed a sprain. I didn't need crutches—the trademark accessory of the "broken" soldier—but I'd still have to hobble around in sneakers for a couple of weeks. For this I was relieved: the sprain could give that bastard blister George a chance to partially heal before getting shoved back into the boots that birthed him. I kept myself safe from further injury for dozens of days after that. All I had to do was focus on not failing any of the qualifying courses or dying of shame and/or heat stroke in the process.

———

Injuries and all, by the eighth week Basic still seems eerily easy, at least compared to the impression I've always gotten of military combat training. The drill sergeants regularly remind us that we are in a "kinder, gentler Army" than they joined. We younger soldiers are lucky, they say, because they can't curse us out or strike us as their drill sergeants had done to them. It also occurs to me that I'm not a typical recruit—I've already been through a vigorous brainwashing in reform school, which employed coercion methods that combined the Twelve Steps of Alcoholics Anonymous with various creative forms of public shaming, verbal abuse, and manual labor. In comparison, the Army's attempts at indoctrination seem almost quaint. The first time I was subjected to the drill sergeants' yelling, I was surprised at and generic it sounded. *No personal insults? No attempts to turn us against one another? No screaming our deepest weaknesses and insecurities into our faces? Amateurs.*

If the drill sergeants are bothered by my apparent immunity to their methods of overt intimidation, they don't show it. My BCGs are fitted with lenses so thick as to nearly obscure my eyes, which makes it easy for them to look past me and choose not to see my poorly-concealed amusement at their shouting. The Army seemed like a smart career move, but I am only willing to sell the government my body—my mind, I am certain, has already been blanketed under a protective anti-war soundtrack. The only class I'd been allowed to attend during my last months at reform school was a folk music class taught by one of the older, harder-lived staff members who'd taken to feeling sorry for me. By the time I'd set off down the road to what I'd hoped was still my home, I'd developed an affinity for Bob Dylan, Joan Baez, and Kris Kristofferson, humming the freshly-committed-to-memory refrain *freedom's just another word for nothing left to lose* as I stretched out a hopeful thumb. At community college, I'd plundered the library for CDs and books about all of them, plus Country Joe McDonald, Joni

Mitchell, Janis Joplin, Woody Guthrie, and every other name I came across, before stumbling into the writings of Jack Kerouac, Neal Cassady, and Hunter S. Thompson, who I knew had also been a military journalist. *Except Hunter Thompson was smart enough to join the Air Force*, I remember bitterly on the most brutal days of Basic.

The drill sergeants ignore me when I hum "The Times, They Are A-Changin'" while on guard duty, or when I use my turn calling marching cadences to lead the platoon in a rousing chorus of "War! What is it good for?" They refuse to acknowledge my decision to name my M16-A2 rifle "Bungalow Bill," and when I explain that my difficulty with marksmanship is because I am a lover of peace and really don't want to have to kill anyone, my drill sergeant's response is a terse, "As long as you qualify, I don't give a shit." I proceed to qualify. He keeps his promise to not give a shit.

"You know you weird, right?" Private Mitchell doesn't mince words, and everyone in our platoon appreciates her for it. She's a tall, mild-mannered soldier from Alabama whose BCGs sit on her dainty nose in a way that lends her an air of bemused authority. It's almost time for lights-out, and I've just expressed disbelief that she's never heard of John Lennon. She looks up from polishing her boots and our nearsighted eyes meet. "Like, you real weird. Singing all them hippie songs and shit."

"Yeah, Mitchell, I know."

"Okay ... as long as you know."

———

One more week to go, and it's finally time for the grenade range. I am exquisitely excited to throw a real grenade, but I do my best to stay outwardly impassive. It's an unfamiliar look for me, but I think I'm pulling it off. At least, until I trip over the grenade pit wall and fall flat on my face, Kevlar helmet smashing not only my glasses, but also my nose.

With nose-blood gushing down the front of my flak jacket, still clutching my grenade to my chest, squinting in the general direction of the bewildered drill sergeant waiting there, I answer with an enthusiastic, "Roger, Drill Sergeant!" when he asks if I still want to complete the training. I pull the pin, lob the grenade in mostly the right direction, barely far enough to qualify. The drill sergeant rolls his eyes. I can tell we're both thinking the same thing: the Army is obviously desperate for recruits.

At least, I console myself, this is a different mistake than the last time I got the eye-roll. That time was in the beginning of Week One. The instructions were to keep one pair of running shoes in our rooms and leave another pair in the duffel bag containing our civilian clothes, to be locked in storage. My stomach had dropped as I remembered I'd failed to get an extra pair of sneakers before leaving home. Standing in line to turn in my bag, fear set in: would this possibly-egregious error be discovered and called out? I'd crept toward the front of the line in a state of near–paralysis, knowing they weren't checking each soldier's bag as they went along, but the instructions were clear—"ONE DADGUM PAIR OF DADGUM RUNNING SHOES IN EACH DADGUM BAG"—and the idea had crossed my mind that the bags might be checked later, revealing my thoughtless indiscretion.

In reform school, the punishment for hiding a mistake was far more severe than for making a mistake in the first place. Students who were deemed dishonest were often forced to begin every sentence, "Hello, my name is _____ and I'm a liar." Even in the first week of Basic I knew that kind of shaming wasn't the Army's way, but I was new enough to this game to still be heart-thumpingly afraid that the "Army Values" I'd just been given to memorize (including Integrity, the "I" in the awkwardly-helpful acronym LDRSHIP) might be enforced in some similarly dramatic fashion.

Nearing the front of the line, I'd decided integrity was the way to go. Amid the din of the concrete-walled room full of irritated privates, I'd stepped up to the fierce-faced Drill Sergeant Maxwell, taken a deep breath, and stepped forward.

"Drill sergeant? I, um, only have one pair of running shoes."

He'd stopped throwing bags into piles ... turned ... and stared at me. *NOOOOOO*, I internally screamed, bracing myself for a verbal beating.

But instead of yelling at me, he'd just let out a long sigh. "Soldier, lemme tell you something."

I waited without breathing for him to continue. Our eyes locked. He lowered his voice, speaking now only to me.

"Soldier, if you ain't cheatin', you ain't tryin'—you got me?" Tongue-tied, I'd nodded. "And if you get caught, you ain't tryin' hard enough. Now gimme that duffel bag and get the fuck outta here."

It was the most useful lesson I'd never learned before—about life, the military, and everything—and he'd laid it on me in less time than it took to lace my boots. It uprooted reform school and displaced the lectures I'd always received from parents, teachers, pastors, and well-meaning mentors on honesty and the right way to live. A deep-rooted proclivity toward integrity might be the right way to live, I realized, but it damn well wasn't the best way to survive. Not even in the "kinder, gentler" Army.

—

None of us can believe it when I finish Basic Combat Training in the prescribed ten weeks. My drill sergeants clearly expected I'd have to redo at least one of the requirements due to my gimpy feet, obvious breathing problems, broken nose, and two black eyes—which, we discovered, is what happens when the most durable eyeglass frames available smash into the bridge of your nose and shatter. They're especially intrigued by my ability to complete the course without the help of my extra-strength BCGs, but, keeping Drill Sergeant Maxwell's words in mind while squinting my way through the final week with my reluctant seeing-eye buddy Small by my side, I see no need to tell the drill sergeants I kept a set of contact lenses in my toiletry kit for just such an emergency. It's a major violation of the rules to wear contacts in training, but we all want me to graduate, so I keep up the charade of blindness with my mouth shut and my head down.

The drill sergeants march us through the parking lot one last time, where charter buses wait to take us on to the next phase of training. As I board the bus headed to Fort Meade, Maryland, and the Defense Information School, I lift my head and, for the first time since breaking my glasses, I relax my nearsighted squint in Drill Sergeant Maxwell's direction. His eyes widen, then relax into the look I've come to recognize as respect. He elbows one of the others, pointing at his eyes and nodding in my direction. They both smirk.

"Thanks, Drill Sergeant!" I call out before hustling into the bus. Maybe Sergeant Baker was right—maybe I'll make a fine soldier, after all.

DEFENSE INFORMATION

"Your writing is too flowery," says the red-inked note at the top of my homework. "This is Army journalism, not Shakespeare." Sergeant First Class Chatswick, unlike me, does not play with words. I stop at his desk after class to make my case.

"Sergeant, I'm just trying to make the story more interesting. It's a feature, not news."

He raises an authoritative eyebrow. "If your opening graf is more than four sentences, it's a book, not a feature."

"But—"

"Look, soldier, this is the Defense Information School. You write what the military tells you to write. And the military did not tell you to write anything about—" he glances at my first page—"the 'starkness of the summer sky' over brigade headquarters."

"Doesn't the Army appreciate alliteration, Sergeant?"

Eyebrow. "I'm pretty sure you know the answer to that stupid question, soldier."

I emit a defeated exhale. "Roger, Sergeant."

"Rewrite it and email it to me tonight and if it's good, I won't deduct any points."

"But Sergeant, tonight we have Phase Five testing. I won't have time."

"If you can write as fast as you can make excuses, you'll be fine."

I mutter a final "Roger," and hustle out the door, down the hall, across the field, and back to Student Company, where Drill Sergeant Billings is waiting.

"PRIVATE! Where the hell have you been? You think I'm gonna hold up phase testing so you can take the long way back to the company?"

"Drill Sergeant, I—"

"Soldier, I don't know why in the ever-loving ass you think I want an answer but you better get your behind upstairs and back down here in the proper uniform before I notice you're not in front of me with the rest of your battle buddies."

I'm short of breath already, but heave myself up the stairs to the third floor, where MacLane is already in her freshly-starched Class A uniform when I get to our room. Straightening the narrow cravat at her buttoned collar, she aims a pointed side-eye in my direction. "Dude, where have you been?"

"Trying to convince Sergeant Chatswick not to dock my grade for writing too creatively." I yank the dark green Class A skirt from my persistently-wobbling wall locker and strip off the camouflage pants I've been sweating in all day. "He says I'm too Shakespearean."

"What does that even mean?" MacLane throws me a pair of nylons.

"I know, right? It's not like I'm writing in iambic pentameter." I pull the hose up my prickly calves and spy a run at the ankle threatening to creep north. "Fuck. Do you think Drill Sergeant Billings will notice this?"

She glances at the offending tear. "Nah."

"Oh, good."

"But Drill Sergeant Hoseman will."

"Dammit. You're right. Fuck me."

"Nobody's fucking you if you don't phase up. Hurry! We have three minutes to be in formation!"

"Almost ready! Hand me my vagina-hat."

MacLane tosses the Class A headgear onto my bed. I check to make sure the Student Company insignia is properly affixed to its front and poke the cap's suggestive folds into place before sliding it securely into the rear waistband of my uniform skirt, where it's barely hidden under the matching jacket.

MacLane points to her wrist, where the digital numbers on her watch must be telling her we're about to be late. "Come ooooon."

"Ready. How do I look?"

She looks me over and frowns. "Like you lost weight since they fitted you for that skirt."

"Fuck it. Let's go."

When we get downstairs, all the other Phase Fours are already in formation, so we take our places at the end of the last squad, avoiding eye contact with Drill Sergeant Billings.

"Is he giving us crazy-eyes?" MacLane whispers through the corner of her mouth.

I give my peripheral a split-second scan over the rows of soldiers ahead of us, where Drill Sergeant Billings is standing completely still at the front of the formation. Staring. At us. "Mm-hm." I don't avert my gaze in time.

"PRIVATE! Are you trying to hide from me?"

"No, Drill Serg—"

"GET TO THE FRONT OF MY FORMATION. Bring your little friend!"

"HOOAH, Drill Sergeant!" By this time, freshly graduated from Basic Combat Training, we have all learned that HOOAH, the Army-invented word that means everything except No, is always the right answer.

MacLane and I exchange a surreptitious cringe. She's the cute one, and yelling, we all deduced way back in Basic, is how drill sergeants flirt. By Week Three of Advanced Individual Training, we've solidly internalized that they love it when we play along by Armying extra hard.

"ARE YOU SMILING, SOLDIER?" Drill Sergeant Billings is hollering at MacLane.

"NEGATIVE, DRILL SERGEANT! I'M JUST FIRED UP, DRILL SERGEANT!"

"WELL YOU BETTER FIX YOUR FACE THEN, PRIVATE!"

"ROGER, DRILL SERGEANT!"

MacLane's smile straightens into a grimace. We both know she's his favorite, but even if she wasn't, being yelled at by Drill Sergeant Billings is like being chased by a toothless chihuahua—a show of strength to compensate for the complete lack of ability to intimidate. He yells like a drill sergeant, but we can tell his heart's not in it. As soon as we're done here, he'll go back to joking with us as usual.

The phase-up test is intended to keep us aware that our ability to feel like humans while in training—such as having the privilege to wear civilian clothes while off-duty, go off-post on the weekends, drink if we're of age, and myriad other illusions of personal autonomy—is entirely dependent on our ability to convince the Army that we are very, very good at acting at all other times like the soldiers we have newly become. All we have to do is spend a few hours racing around like spastic cockroaches with our drill sergeants barking orders at us while they make an unconvincing effort to look less entertained than they are.

Yelling! Uniform inspection! Push-ups! Sit-ups! Now run up the stairs and change uniforms! Back down for inspection! Yelling! Push-ups! Sit-ups! Why you look so sweaty, soldier? Answer questions about obscure Army regulations! Fix your face! Yelling! Pushups! Change uniforms! Disassemble and reassemble this weapon! Get outside and run around the building! Back inside! QUICKLIER! Yelling! Push-ups! Didn't I say fix your face?! DO PUSH-UPS! Okay you're done now HERE take your civvies and GET OUT OF MY COMMON AREA BEFORE I CHANGE MY MIND.

Scurrying out of the common area and back up the two flights of stairs to our room, MacLane and I collapse in soldierly giggles on our beds.

"Bahahaha! They're so cute when they try to intimidate us!"

"I KNOW! It's like they think they're infantry drill sergeants!"

"RIGHT? Did you see Drill Sergeant Billings almost laugh when he was yelling at Towers?"

"And then yell at her more when she almost laughed back at him?"

"YES holy shit that was HILARIOUS."

Towers pokes her head into our room, already decked out in her newly-reacquired Friday-night civilian clothes. "YOU GUYS. I ALMOST LOST MY SHIT."

"WE KNOW!"

"This shit is a JOKE!"

"For REAL!"

"Okay but why are you two still in uniform? Come onnnn, get changed and let's find someone to take us to the bar!"

"Um, when did you turn twenty-one?"

"The other Phase Fives told me Hammer Jack's is eighteen and up. You only need to be twenty-one to buy drinks and I'm *pretty* sure we can find someone to do that for us. Hurry up or we'll have to take the bus!"

MacLane and I jump back into action, still sweat-faced but now moving with renewed purpose. In thirty seconds our beds are covered with wrinkled clothes that smell like they've been sitting in the bottom of a duffel bag for four months, because that is exactly where they've been. We were bussed to Fort Meade directly from Basic Training, and the bags bearing our civvies haven't been opened since we stumbled off the buses that dumped us off at Basic for ten weeks.

"Is this shirt still cute? Or do I look like I wore it all weekend already?"

"Ummm … you kinda look like you wore it all week. Even to PT."

"Okay, okay. How 'bout this?"

"Sliiiightly better. Here, use my iron. And this Febreze."

"Now I smell like a sofa."

"Better than smelling like Fort Jackson and BO."

"Good point. You don't have any makeup, do you?"

"YES. Don't you?"

"NO. Why would I bring makeup to Basic Combat Training?"

"Because you knew you'd be coming here afterward? I mean, why wouldn't you? Just in case?"

"In case of what? In case I'm ordered to look feminine? Is that how they do it in the National Guard?"

"LOOK, I DON'T KNOW. I COULDN'T HELP IT."

MacLane is from San Antonio, the daughter of a white Texan father and a Japanese mother, and is objectively beautiful, with or without makeup. Still, I believe her when she says she couldn't resist the compulsion to stick a full array of cosmetics into her bag while packing for Basic. She's also been drilling with her Guard unit since her senior year of high school, and heard about the lax environment of public affairs specialist training at Fort Meade's Student Company long before we all arrived here. She's younger than I am, but in this regard at least, I consider her my elder.

"Instruct me in the ways of presentability, Obi Wan."

"You're a dork. Here, use whatever you want."

I'm halfway done with my second eye when I remember the feature I'm supposed to be rewriting. I let out a groan. "Uuugh. How important do you think it is that I get those points back for that article Sergeant Chatswick was up my ass about?"

She's already finished getting ready to go and has one foot out the steel-framed door. The other one is tapping the concrete floor impatiently. "Dude, I'm sure it's not a big deal. Just make the next one extra-boring."

"You're probably right. All the rest of my grades have been fine. Even though writing Army news is so easy it's almost hard."

"Like Sergeant Chatswick says, keep it at a fifth-grade reading level—our target audience is soldiers."

"Ha, yeah. Soldiers. Like us."

MacLane rolls her eyes. "Not exactly like us. Don't forget we had to get that 110 GT score just to get into this MOS."

"True, there's that." The General Technical score on the Army aptitude test tells recruiters how potential enlistees' word knowledge, paragraph comprehension, and arithmetic reasoning measure up. The Defense Information School requires public affairs soldiers to have a higher GT score to qualify for our military occupational specialty than our counterparts need for a combat-related MOS, although we're highly discouraged from talking about that while we are, for example, interviewing them for morale-boosting articles. We are journalists, our instructors are fond of telling us. We must remain professional.

"Are you almost ready? Let's gooooo."

I dab at my hastily-applied lipstick with a tissue and give myself a once-over in the cloudy wall-locker mirror before slamming the door shut and clicking the padlock into place. "Wow, that worked. I look like a lady!"

MacLane throws me a critical eye. "Imagine if that lipstick was actually your color. Come on, Towers is waiting!"

———

Monday comes faster than it did last weekend, when we were still restricted to post and spent our evenings watching movies in the Student Company barracks. Sergeant First Class Chatswick directs a disapproving stink-eye at me as I skulk into the classroom.

"I didn't get your revisions, Private."

"I know, Sergeant."

"It wasn't because you phased up, was it?"

"Ahhhm …"

"You and MacLane need to come see me at the end of the day. Roger?"

"Roger, Sergeant."

We spend the morning working on the proper format for a news story. Sergeant First Class Chatswick reads us a scenario: "A combat operation in Kabul, Afghanistan, results in two casualties for the U.S. and ten for the enemy, along with the recovery of a stockpile of weapons including three rocket-propelled grenade launchers, twenty grenades, ten AK-47s, and three hundred rounds of ammunition, as well as a thousand U.S. dollars in cash. The goal of the mission was to capture a well-known Taliban operative, but unfortunately the operative received a tip and disappeared before U.S. troops arrived. As the public affairs specialist who both covered and photographed the operation, you've got quotes from the officers who directed the operation, as well as from the soldiers on the ground who are shaken by the loss of their comrades, and blame the intelligence officers for failing to provide accurate information. Your photos are of the weapons stockpile, the casualties on both sides, and the soldiers carrying out the mission. What angle do you take for your article, which photos do you submit, and whose quotes do you include?"

Hands go up. Sergeant Chatswick calls on a bespectacled Marine gunnery sergeant with a high-and-tight who always sits in the front row. He's being re-classed to a new MOS after a combat injury disqualified him from the infantry, and I'm nearly certain he hates all of us. It's hard to tell, though, because he gets to class early every day and never turns around. "What do you think, Martin?"

"Start by talking about the weapons that were retrieved. Focus on the successful part of the mission."

MacLane is next. "Use the quotes from the command team about how competent the soldiers were."

A petty officer in blindingly clean Navy whites raises his hand. "Send the photos of the weapons cache and the mission-in-progress."

"Talk about the bravery of the KIAs," suggests the Coastie with the perpetually cheerful disposition.

"Do we know the names of the casualties?" comes a voice from the back of the room. The voice belongs to Golden, a fellow Army Private First Class who rarely volunteers.

"Uh, we might," Sergeant First Class Chatswick acknowledges. "But what do we do before we publish them?"

"Make sure the families have been notified," we all respond in unison.

"How about the casualties on the other side?" Golden is uncharacteristically talkative today.

Sergeant First Class Chatswick shifts from one foot to the other at the front of the room. "Um, no, I don't think we have those names."

"Are we going to?"

"Uh, probably not."

"So we just write that there were ten enemy casualties?"

"Ah, yes. That's correct."

Golden sits quietly with a thoughtful expression. After a moment, he nods. "Okay. Roger that."

The Coastie raises her hand. "We don't mention the intelligence error at all, right?"

Sergeant Chatswick sighs. "What do you think?"

"No?"

"Correct. Now, everyone, take twenty minutes to write your articles and then we'll go over them together."

After class, MacLane and I stay behind as directed. Sergeant Chatswick sits on the front of his desk, a weary half-grimace on his pale face. He rubs his temples, ruffling his neatly-trimmed salt-and-pepper sideburns. "All right you two, here's the deal. You obviously spend a lot of time together, yes?"

MacLane and I nod. "We're roommates, Sergeant," we say almost in unison.

He sighs. "Of course you are. Okay, so this shouldn't be difficult." He raises his head heavily and turns to me. "You need help with your loquacity. I know you know what that word means because I'm pretty sure you tried to use it in your feature about the new commanding general." I smirk. He lifts an eyebrow. I fix my face. "MacLane needs help with her sentence structure. You both give me a headache, so you're going to work together until I'm satisfied with your articles. Got it?"

"Roger, Sergeant," we answer, actually in unison this time.

"Christ. All right, Tweedledee and Tweedledum. Get out of here and get to work. And stop all that damn giggling. This is the Defense Information School, not your high school newspaper."

"Roger, Sergeant!" we chirp. We barely make it out the door before the damn giggling commences.

"Hahaha! I saw you smirk!" MacLane gasps between guffaws.

"Oh shut up, you would have too if he'd given you that look!"

"No way, I know how to keep a straight face. What the fuck is loquacity?"

"It means I use too many words. It's not my fault DINFOS doesn't appreciate all of them."

"Um, considering they shortened Defense Information School to DINFOS, I don't know why you're surprised."

"Ugh. I'm not surprised. Just annoyed."

"Well if it makes you feel any better, I think my sentence structure is fine."

"I mean, it probably is. But just give me your articles and I'll fix whatever's wrong and I'll give you mine and you can tell me which words you don't know so I can take 'em out and then he'll be off both our asses by the weekend."

"Perfect."

"At least we finally phased up. I can't wait to get off post and away from these crazy people."

"Four days till Friday. We got this."

———

Our plan succeeds brilliantly. By the end of the week, Sergeant Chatswick is satisfied with MacLane's snappy sentences and applies his stamp of approval to what I've taken to calling my "bore-ticles." When Friday night finally arrives, we secure a ride to the bar and gleefully prepare to flee the confines of Student Company.

"Are you signing out overnight, or coming back?" Specialist Kasey is on control-point guard at the company's front desk every weekend, ever since she failed out of the course and got stuck waiting for the next cycle of classes to begin. Her eyes, set in a permanent glare, shoot hate-lasers at MacLane and me.

"Coming back."

She scowls at the sign-out sheet. "Make sure you're not late for bed-check."

"We know, we know, byyyye!"

The bar is wall-to-wall with blatantly-underage bodies by the time we arrive, every hand in the room holding a plastic cup full of something that, judging by the sea of swaying minors, is definitely alcoholic. MacLane and I smile sweetly at two boys with wrist-bands displaying their legality, and when they hand us our cups, Friday night officially begins. MacLane disappears to the far side of the dance floor with the goatee'd guido who gave her the drink, I position myself closer to the bar and get to know the ginger who bought mine, and by the time our ride taps us on the shoulder to let us know it's time to get back to the barracks for bed-check, we're four drinks in and have almost entirely forgotten we're in the Army.

"Dammit!" MacLane slurs. "I don't waaaanna go back."

"Me eeeeither," I whine. "This guy I've been dancing with's got a room in town ..."

"But we have to get back for bed-check," MacLane moans. "Unless ..."

"Unless what?"

MacLane straightens herself and grins. "Unless we call one of the new Phase Fours and ask her to stuff our beds."

"Hahaha! Dude. You are drunk."

"I know, but …"

"Wait—really? Are you for serious?"

Her grin widens. "Phillips owes me a favor since I took her fire-guard shift."

"You're insane!"

"Come on, you know Drill Sergeant Billings barely looks into the room!"

"We will be in SO. MUCH. TROUBLE."

"Not if Phillips does it right!"

I try to give her a stern look of disapproval, but four rounds of Jack and Coke deny me the ability to focus on even one of the two sets of eyes I now see on MacLane's face.

"Fuck. We can't go back to the barracks wasted like this anyway. Fine. Call her."

MacLane lets out a squeal and pulls out the new Nokia 3310 cell phone she's just acquired from one of the vendors on-post. She dials the number to the pay phone on our barracks floor and I can barely hear her over the thumping club music as she asks the fire guard to put Phillips on the phone. A few minutes later, she hangs up with a shit-eating smile.

"She's doing it! She's stuffing our beds!"

"Oh my god, really?"

"YES!"

"AAHH!"

"I KNOW!"

"Well … fuck it!"

"Yes! Let's stay out!"

"Okay!"

———

Drill Sergeant Billings is standing in the barracks doorway when we make our appearance in the harsh light of Saturday, wearing smudged makeup and Friday night's clothes. His trademark crazy-eyes look as though they are about to jump out of his head and punch us in the face. "Well I'll be goddamned. If it ain't the smartest soldiers in Student Company. Welcome back."

MacLane turns on her trusty charm. "Heyyyy Drill Sergeant Billings."

"I know you did not just 'hey Drill Sergeant Billings' me. START PUSHING."

We drop to the ground and commence our punitive push-ups. MacLane speaks up, still facing the floor. "Drill Sergeant, we were just—"

"If that sentence doesn't end with 'acting like goddamn FOOLS' you can save your breath for a full day of push-ups, soldier! Now get up and get out of my goddamn sight before I go and PT you to death and get my ass in trouble."

"Roger, Drill Sergeant!"

Battling our crippling hangovers, MacLane and I take the two flights of stairs two at a time, fling open the door to our room, and plop onto our beds, whose covers have been ripped off to reveal the piles of uniforms and linens that Phillips decided looked satisfactorily like our sleeping forms.

"Hey, she didn't do a bad job," MacLane observes. "Nice proportions."

"Seriously. Yours looks like it even has the right size hips."

Phillips appears in the doorway, eyes darting down the hall behind her. "Oh my god you guys, I am so sorry."

"Don't worry about it." MacLane walks over and gives her shoulder an awkward pat that I think is intended to be comforting. "You did good."

"Really? Because Drill Sergeant Billings—"

"He's not your problem. Relax, you won't get in trouble. We won't tell him it was you."

"But who will you say it was?"

"We'll say we did it ourselves before leaving."

"You know he won't belie—"

"Don't worry. We're already in trouble, no need to drag you down with us."

"Are you sure?"

"Of course. Relax. You're fine."

Phillips takes what I'm guessing to be her first deep breath of the day. "Okay, if you're sure."

"We're sure! Go, have a fun Saturday. We'll deal with Drill Sergeant Billings."

Phillips backs out of the door and takes off down the hall. MacLane and I sit in silence for what feels like an hour.

"We're fucked, huh?" she eventually emits.

"Oh, dude. We're all the way fucked. In the ass. With no lube."

"Do you think they'll keep us from graduating? My unit's gonna be pissed if they paid for me to go to AIT and I don't graduate."

"I mean, your grades are fine, right?"

"Yeah …"

"So are mine. Hopefully they'll let us get away with administrative discipline."

"I guess we'll find out when Drill Sergeant Waltman gets in on Monday."

"Yup."

"Ugh, that guy's a dick."

"Seriously. He tried to make me give him my Bob Dylan tickets when they kept us on post to do that ruck march last Sunday."

MacLane rolls her eyes. "Bob Dylan sucks anyway."

I stick out my tongue and raspberry my response at her. "You're entitled to your opinion."

"Well he *does* suck."

"I kind of hate that Drill Sergeant Waltman has good taste in music."

"He doesn't. Neither do you."

"You're so nice when you're hung over."

"Nicer than Drill Sergeant Waltman when he's in a good mood."

"That is definitely true. Did I tell you how he laughed at me when I told him I was supposed to go to airborne school?"

"No. But I'm not surprised."

"I told him my recruiter said even though it wasn't in my contract, I'd still be able to get it taken care of when I got to AIT."

"No wonder he laughed. Your recruiter was full of shit."

"As I've discovered. He also told me I needed to sign up for five years instead of four to get this MOS."

"Ha! You could've signed up for three. Like half the people here."

"A fact of which I am now painfully aware."

"I'd have laughed at you too."

"You're an asshole. Take a nap. When you're ready to be nice we'll figure out how to deal with this mess. Who knows, maybe it'll be fine."

MacLane falls back onto her pillow with a tritoned sigh. "That was a fun night though, huh?"

"Wicked fun. Rest up. We'll be all right."

—

Monday arrives and with it comes Drill Sergeant Waltman, Student Company's senior drill, a tall, barrel-chested, small-headed man whose face always looks like it's about to either tell a dirty joke or start a fight or both. MacLane and I are hustling through the common area on our way to formation when he thunders through the door.

"WELL, WELL, WELL," he booms. "DUMB AND DUMBER."

We stop dutifully in our tracks, stand at parade-rest, and wait.

"I heard about your fuckin' genius move over the weekend. Did you two really think you were gonna get away with that shit?"

We are well aware that there is no right answer here. MacLane speaks up anyway. "Drill Sergeant—"

"SAVE IT FOR MY OFFICE. Be there at 1700. Before you go to the chow hall. If my dinner has to wait, yours does too."

"Roger, Drill Sergeant," we intone in one miserable voice.

"Fuckin' privates," I hear him mutter not-quite-under his breath as he strides away. "Goddamn fuckin' privates."

MacLane and I stay stock-still until he disappears behind his office door. "We might be fuckin' privates but we're probably better writers than him," I retort in a hissing whisper.

"Probably? Definitely. Fuck him, let's get to class."

——

By the time 1700 rolls around, word of our weekend exploits has gotten around DINFOS, and we've both become so visibly tense that the other soldiers are asking us if we're sick.

"No, we just need to go see Drill Sergeant Waltman after classes."

"Aaaah. Oof. Good luck," they say with sympathy. "We'll pray for you."

When we show up at the senior drill's office, Drill Sergeant Billings is there with Drill Sergeant Hoseman, an angry-faced, sinewy woman with stringy blonde hair and a pre-cancerous tan who hates female soldiers and has made no secret of her specific disdain for the unquestionably attractive MacLane. Drill Sergeant Hoseman's expression is the closest to happy that I've ever seen it, which can only mean something is about to make MacLane and me very sad.

"You girls think you're pretty clever, huh," she spits out of a sideways smile. "Stuffing the bed. You must think we're all as stupid as you are."

Not stupid enough to answer that, I hear my brain retort. We remain silent.

Drill Sergeant Waltman makes his entrance, slamming the door behind him. "Okay, Privates. You ready for the good news?"

"Hooah, Drill Sergeant," we take turns mumbling.

He snorts. "Sure ya are. Okay, here's what's gonna happen. You're both back down to Phase Four and you're gonna stay there for the rest of the cycle. You'll turn in your civilian clothes and get them back after graduation."

MacLane and I conduct a split-second exchange of glances. Her eyes flash, and I know we're both thinking the same thing: *They're gonna let us graduate.*

Drill Sergeant Waltman is still talking. "You lose your off-post privileges and you will BOTH be subject to administrative discipline in the form of a company-grade Article 15 under the Uniform Code of Military Justice."

Not field-grade! I mentally celebrate, willing my face to stay fixed. Field-grade Article 15s follow a soldier's entire military career—company-grade disciplinary records disappear once we leave the company where we're assigned. *Bullet dodged.*

"You will maintain your grades and await the processing of your Article 15s. You will wear your pistol-belts with attached canteens every day like the rest of the Phase Fours. You will NOT LEAVE THIS POST. IS THAT CLEAR."

"Yes, Drill Sergeant!"

"I said IS THAT CLEAR."

"HOOAH, DRILL SERGEANT!"

"Now get the fuck out of my office before you stink it up with your stupid."

We straighten to the position of attention, exiting in exactly the way we were repetitively instructed during our first day here, and make haste to the chow hall, where dinner is almost done being served.

"Company-grade!" MacLane blurts as we plop our trays onto the table. "Fuck, we're lucky!"

"OH MY GOD."

"That was CLOSE. I wonder if they'll take any of our pay."

"I don't even care. I'm just glad they're letting us graduate."

My mouth is full of Sysco-truck cheeseburger, so all I can do is vigorously nod. "Mmf-HMM."

"I wonder how long it'll take to process."

"Who cares! I will miss my civvies, though."

"Yeah. Oh well. At least they're not recycling us."

"That would be the worst."

"Whew. I can breathe again."

"Just be careful. Drill Sergeant Hoseman is gonna be watching us even closer with those beady little eyes."

"Let her watch. All we have to do is keep our grades up in Sergeant Chatswick's class and we'll be out before she can fuck with us."

—

The crunchy Maryland fall makes way for a bitter winter by the last week of November, and it's all I can do to stay on top of my increasingly demanding workload. Having mastered my news-writing, feature-writing, sportswriting, and photography blocks of instruction, all that remains of the thirteen-week Basic Journalism Course (which has just been redesignated as the "Basic Public Affairs Course-Writer" for maximum syntactical irony) is graphic design, newspaper layout, and media relations.

"You're not going to be expected to do much media-liaison work right away," Sergeant First Class Chatswick announces. "That's mostly for commissioned officers, not enlisted folks. But you need to know how to interact with reporters and instruct other service members on how to do the same. The last thing your units need is Joe talking to Chris from CNN about the mission being a disaster."

Don't let Joe talk to reporters, I scrawl in my notebook.

To unwind at the end of the day, I log onto one of the shared Student Company computers and scroll absently through *The Onion*'s website. "Bush Won't Stop Asking Cheney If We Can Invade Yet," reads one headline. I snort and click the link. "WASHINGTON, D.C.—Vice-President Dick Cheney issued a stern admonishment to President Bush Tuesday, telling the over-eager chief executive that he didn't want to hear 'so much as the word "Iraq" for the rest of the day.'"

I've been so busy learning to expertly-craft Defense Information that I haven't been closely following the actual news. *There's no way we'll go to Iraq*, I tell myself. *We're too busy in Afghanistan.* As I scan the rest of the article, it's hard for me to believe this is a prospect worth taking seriously enough to turn into satire. I sigh and log out. Leaving the computer room, I run directly into Drill Sergeant Waltman.

"HEY SOLDIER!"

I fix my face and stand at parade-rest. "ROGER, DRILL SERGEANT!"

"HOW DO YOU FEEL ABOUT GOING TO KUWAIT?"

I freeze. *Was he watching me web-browse? This has to be a trick question. Drill sergeants don't care about feelings.* I go with the safest possible answer. "R-r-roger, Drill Sergeant?"

Drill Sergeant Waltman lets out what I think is supposed to be a laugh but sounds more like a bark. "HA. CARRY ON, SOLDIER."

I carry on, dismissing my confusion. I have an assignment to finish.

———

It's the day before graduation, and MacLane and I still haven't received our respective official Article 15s. We're both getting nervous.

"What if they make us stay after graduation to be processed?" She worries at me on the way to our final class. "My unit will be pissed!"

"Mine too," I fret back, picking up my pace. "I just found out I'm getting sent to Georgia. The 3rd Infantry Division."

"Ew. I heard that place suuuucks. I'm glad I get to go home to Texas."

"You were right to go Guard. Active-duty gets extra-fucked, from what I hear."

"Yep, I hear that too."

"Thanks."

"Anytime."

As we take our places in class, Sergeant First Class Chatswick's expression brightens. "My two most-improved soldiers! Ready to graduate?"

"Roger, Sergeant!"

"Excited to get rid of us, Sergeant?"

He chuckles. "Surprisingly, no. You two have kept me on my toes. I wouldn't mind keeping you around."

I let out a snort. "You might have a chance, Sergeant. We still haven't had our Article 15s processed."

"I was wondering why you were still in those pistol belts every day. What was it you did, again?"

"Stayed out overnight without authorization and stuffed our beds for bed check."

"Ha! Ah, you privates. Always good for a laugh."

"Happy to entertain, Sergeant."

He grins, an expression we've seen more frequently as the end of the course has drawn near. His neatly-trimmed sideburns seem to have acquired more salt than pepper over the past three months. "You'll be fine once you get to your duty station. The drill sergeants here are just concerned with keeping you in line till you get through your training."

"MacLane's in the Guard. She's going back to Texas to be part-civilian again."

"How about you?"

"Fort Stewart."

"Georgia! Isn't that the 3rd ID?"

"That's what I hear."

A thoughtful look crosses his face. "I hear the 3rd ID is about to get pretty busy."

"Drill Sergeant Waltman asked me how I felt about going to Kuwait."

"Oh did he? And what did you say?"

"I said HOOAH."

Sergeant Chatswick's smile fades a bit. "Well, that was the right answer, I suppose. Just keep your head down, all right?"

"Roger, Sergeant. That's the plan."

"You'll be fine," he repeats, and I nod, wondering if he's trying to convince me or himself. "You'll be fine."

—

Drill Sergeant Waltman calls MacLane and me into his office after graduation. His face is tired. Drill Sergeant Hoseman is standing next to his desk, her eyes burning with annoyance.

"Well, Privates, you're in luck."

Standing at parade-rest, we wait for the opposite to be true.

"Your paperwork got held up too long at battalion. Turns out Private First Class MacLane here happens to be National Guard, and her unit isn't interested in paying for her to stay here any longer to get her Article 15 processed."

MacLane and I exchange confused looks.

Drill Sergeant Waltman continues, "So we have to send her home without it. And because the two of you did the same thing, we can't keep one of you here if the other gets to leave."

My mouth falls slightly open. I fix my face.

"What I'm saying is neither of you are getting an Article 15. You can thank the Army's incredible competence."

MacLane and I stand in stunned silence.

"Now get the fuck out of here before I find something wrong with you."

We straighten to the position of attention, still in shock. "Hooah, Drill Sergeant," I hear myself say and MacLane echo.

"Happy graduation, soldiers. Good luck in the real Army. You're gonna need it."

The office door clicks behind us once we're through it. MacLane and I stop on the other side of it and stare at each other.

"Did—did that just happen?" she squeaks.

"Um, I … I think it did." I can barely get the words out.

She bursts into a fit of giggles. They're contagious. Before Drill Sergeant Waltman can hear us, we take off across the common area and back up the stairs to our room. I pull off my Phase Four pistol belt for the final time and throw it to the ground.

"Oh, man." I gasp for breath between unrestrained guffaws. "Is it just me, or is the Army kind of … bullshit?"

MacLane nods, finally beginning to regain her composure, tears of relieved hilarity still wet on her cheeks. "Oh yeah. Complete bullshit."

———

MacLane and I hug goodbye for a final time as I hoist my duffel bag onto the bus that will take me to the airport and then to Fort Stewart.

"Have fun in Texas!"

"Have fun in Georgia!"

"You mean, Kuwait?"

"Ha! Probably."

We agree to keep our respective heads down. I board the bus and wave out the window. We pull away from Student Company and I let out a long breath that feels as though it, like me, has been waiting three months to escape.

THE BEIGE MILE

We're in the checkout line at the Shoppette when I feel the mushrooms kick in. Nicole and I catch each other's eye, barely suppressing a dangerous case of the giggle-snorts. It's time to go.

"Dude," she says in a low, meaningful tone. This is, after all, a convenience store on a military base—*our* military base. Getting caught while high on psilocybin is not an option, even if we *weren't* in uniform and it *was* Saturday night. But then, what soldier doesn't love to take an idiot chance or few for fun?

"I know," I whisper back. We've given ourselves thirty minutes. We must be dragging ass because now, under the Shoppette's bright lights, surrounded by fellow military personnel, everything in the store is shimmering. "We're almost done here, just stay calm."

She tugs at her University of Michigan sweatshirt and glances nervously around the store. "I hope nobody talks to me."

The words leave her mouth like some kind of cosmic ice-breaker—not even a minute passes before the soldier behind us in line decides now would be a perfect time to make Nicole's acquaintance.

"Nice sweatshirt," he says in what he must think is a flirtatious way. My friend's eyes flash over to me and then down at the ground. She mumbles a terse, "Thanks."

"Are you from Michigan?" Unsurprisingly, he is not fluent in reading body language.

"Yeah." Her tone wills him to stop trying and that, too, fails.

"Oh." He pauses. "So ... what are you doing here in Savannah?"

Nicole looks down at her sweatshirt, basketball shorts and sneakers before shooting me one raised eyebrow and a look of utter confusion. Everyone knows the only people who can access this shop are military members and their families. I'm a bit overweight and probably could pass for a family member, but Nicole, cut like a personal trainer, with her hair tightly wrapped in a regulation bun, is undeniably a soldier. Her measured response: "I'm ... in the Army?"

She answers him with as little eye contact as possible, trying to figure out if more words are necessary. She looks to me for help. I have no better suggestion. Before things can get any more awkward, the cashier saves us.

"NEXT."

We pay for our snacks with record-breaking speed and flee the Shoppette, barely making it out of the parking lot before the snort-laughs overtake us.

"Dude," Nicole gasps. "Was that ... a stupid question?"

"Yes," I squeak back, barely breathing, words coming out in choppy spurts. "Holyshit ... thatwas ... soclose."

Usually we're more responsible, but tonight we've been careless. Going out in public to a military convenience store right after eating a peanut-butter-mushroom sandwich? A few months ago, we would never have been so bold. It's going to be a challenge getting back to the barracks without attracting undue attention—not that we want to be there, but our options are limited. That's how we've ended up in this predicament in the first place.

———

Waking up every day surrounded by asbestos-filled brick walls and leaky ceilings, I find it damn near impossible to feel like life has any special purpose. Living in the barracks has come to require significant substance abuse. I first realized this the weekend I moved in, when the dingy hall filled up with loud, drunken soldiers and gave way to scenes of debauchery that would make frat boys blush. I've never lived in a college dorm, but have visited enough of my friends' rooms to compare them to my current home, and now know that college kids can never party like soldiers—not without the depth of hopelessness and despair that can only be achieved through fully internalizing the fact of being government property. Students drink like they're celebrating their freedom. Soldiers drink like we're trying to forget we've lost ours. Sometimes it works.

I come home to the barracks after a long day of creating morale-boosting, newsy-looking articles for my fellow troops and I smell the alcohol fumes and cigarette smoke before I even walk in. I brace myself for either a hilarious scene, a horrible one, or some bizarre combination of the two. At the closest end of the long, littered, tobacco-stained hallway we all call the Beige Mile, Reardon is leaning out his doorway gripping a bottle of tequila: "Everyone's doing shots!" A few steps further, there's Payne, propped mostly upright by his doorframe, a handle of Hennessy dragging him closer to the floor. Next door, Spriggs and Warner, each on their fifth PBR, are hosting any who happen to stumble in. Another two doors down, the loud one whose real name is forgotten in favor of "Toe," chugs whiskey while his TV blares the most graphically abusive porn available. His next-door neighbor, the parachute rigger I've recently been sporadically sleeping with, cracks a joke about getting married so we can get a housing allowance and move out.

The only way I can tell the night is young? My shoes aren't sticking to the floor yet, and nobody has tried to kidding-not-kiddingly tie up my ankles and wrists—but it's only a matter of time, in a barracks full of inebriated soldiers with pockets full of zip-ties and no detectable morals.

As far as getting obliterated enough to misplace my room goes, booze probably could do the trick on its own without breaking a sweat. Eventually though, the same old self-destructive behaviors become boring. It would be better for all involved if we were allowed to smoke a joint or few after work, but other than coffee and sugar, alcohol is the only drug we can keep flowing steadily and legally through our bloodstream without risking a life-wrecking, random urinalysis. Sure, we take chances on weed from time to time. Some brave ones even dabble in cocaine, but there are very few non-alcoholic substances that are guaranteed not to screw our chances of passing a drug test, so as far as I'm concerned, any that come my way are worth a try.

—

The first mushrooms were dropped into my waiting hands by the Rangers in the neighboring barracks. It didn't take me long to find out that when you need anything illegal in the Army, you always go to the soldiers with the weakest survival instinct—if there are no Special Forces around, Rangers will do. For my initiatory trip, Reardon down the hall gave me a gift, just in case I needed an emergency intervention: a DVD of The Wizard of Oz with the entire Dark Side Of The Moon album laid over the movie, perfectly synchronized. I'm sure he thought it would ferry me away to a land of magic and wonder, but by the time Dorothy was halfway over the rainbow, I was so paranoid that someone would discover what I was doing that I couldn't even relax enough to decide whether I thought Pink Floyd had made the album match the movie on purpose. The walls closed in on me. When I cautiously left my room to knock on Reardon's door for moral support, the fluorescent lights in the barracks hallway were blinding. The Beige Mile seemed to stretch on for several iridescent beige miles as I made my way to the room at the opposite end of the hall, stretched out a hand that looked like mine, and knocked. He appeared behind the door with half-shut eyes.

"Whayya want."

Why was I there? Oh, that's right. "So, um, are we sure Glinda is the *Good* Witch?"

"Whaa?" He rubbed his eyes with a meaty fist. "Dude, go to sleep."

"Is that an option?"

He grunted. "Just wait it out," he mumbled, flopping back onto his bunk. "Sorry you're not having fun."

It had taken me hours to find my way to dreamland, tossing and turning with visions of the Lollipop Guild dancing through my head until I passed out from exhaustion and when I woke up, the barracks were even more depressing than usual. As confused as it was by the new experience, though, my tripping mind had awakened my sober mind to the idea that underage drinking was not the only way for me to flee the monotony of military life. Aside from the insomnia, the experience had been exciting—colors were more vibrant, mundane activities were more interesting, and life just seemed … funnier. All I had to do was find a dependable source, and I could have a psychedelic escape hatch any time I wanted.

But the idea of finding a regular connection to all-natural psilocybin seemed ludicrous—I was in the middle of Savannah, with few friends outside the military and a junior-high education when it came to finding drugs. I had barely met anyone who lived outside our base, and the Rangers who'd gotten me my first dose had since deployed to Iraq. I knew better than to start asking around. My only option was to keep my eyes and ears peeled and hope for luck. After a few months of hanging out at the local head shop and lurking around bars frequented by Savannah's small but noticeable population of art students, I had just about given up. Then luck showed up where I least expected it—Pizza Hut.

Burnt out on drunken hook-ups with our fellow soldiers, my roommate and I had devised a number of creative ways of meeting men who weren't in the military. Sometimes we'd go out to the clubs and dance with anyone who didn't have a regulation haircut. Sometimes we went to church. And sometimes we ordered pizza to flirt with the delivery boy. It wasn't exactly the classiest way to catch a civilian, but both of us agreed we'd rather put in the effort to date someone who'd been trained to deliver pizza in a half-hour, instead of yet another who'd been trained to kill.

That was how we met Matt, a skinny, shaggy-haired Savannah boy who, after finishing his pizza delivery shifts, spent summer nights in local cow pastures.

"Tipping cows?" I'd asked him the first night, half-joking.

"Nope," he'd grinned. "Flipping cow *turds*."

My face had given away my confusion. He'd added helpfully, "You know, for the mushrooms."

I put the pieces together. "Because mushrooms grow …"

"… in cow shit. Yep."

Matt and his girlfriend Sara, a tanned brunette with a loud laugh and a septum piercing, were pros at the mushroom hunt. I got to know them both over the next few months, dropping by their apartment to see half the floor covered with newspaper, upon which scores of the fungi, nicknamed "brownies" for their earthy color and fertilizer, would be drying.

Even with the floor halfway hidden by drugs, it was still more spacious and pleasant than the barracks and contained far fewer drunk misogynists at any given time. Matt and Sara smoked enough weed to get my whole battalion stoned, and their apartment was a perfect place to hang out if you wanted an effective contact high, which I always did. After a while I'd notice I was watching them weigh out baggies of mushrooms like it was reality TV.

There would always come a time in our days together when one of them would offer me a few little caps and stems to take home. Sure, it was illegal, but my chances of being caught were laughably slim. Besides, I'm a twenty-year-old Private First Class with a penchant for risk-taking, a closet full of flowy skirts, and a deep, unflinching love for the music of The Sixties. What do I say—no? How rude. So a tiny baggie would be produced, mushrooms dropped in, and back I'd go to the barracks, caps in hand. That was the easy part. The next step would be more challenging: I had to find myself a buddy.

Having gleaned from my maiden voyage that embarking alone was not the best plan, I realized it was crucial to take any future journeys with a trusted friend. Matt and Sara were abstaining for the time being, and although I didn't always make the wisest decisions, I did know better than to ask anyone in my unit, or at the club, or in the Bible study group I'd joined a few months earlier (another botched attempt to try and meet someone nice who didn't own combat boots). I decided I'd prefer my buddy to be another woman—but who?

I don't have any women co-workers—not that I would have been interested in tripping with one—and my roommate, though equipped with the alcohol tolerance equivalent of a linebacker, is vocally not into that kind of thing. The only civilian women I know are from church, so it would have to be another soldier. But there are only two other women on our barracks floor. One of them, Henderson, keeps mostly to herself in the barracks. I consider this a sign of her superior intelligence, and although we get along fine, I have a feeling that eating mushrooms with the weirdo white girl across the hall isn't on her bucket list.

That left Nicole. Although she lives in the room next to mine, she isn't in the Headquarters Company with the rest of us on the first floor. She's a medic, which to my mind means that if anything goes terribly wrong, she'll be the right one to have with me when it does. Never having met a medic yet who wasn't up for some casual drug experimentation, I suspected she'd be on board. On returning from Matt and Sara's, I knocked on her door and held out the baggie. Her eyes lit up.

"When?"

We'd decided to do it the following Friday, after work, which would give us maximum recovery time. Beyond that, we didn't have much of a plan—well, other than not getting caught. Being soldiers, we weren't trained to think. On instinct alone, we made the call to use the mushrooms as day-old-pizza toppings and then go for a walk in the humid Georgia July evening. Under different circumstances, our walk would've been at the beach, in the woods or even in some quiet neighborhood, but unfortunately we didn't have different circumstances. Unless we wanted to drive or be driven somewhere, our options were limited to the trippiest place imaginable within walking distance—the vicinity of the barracks. First, we'd have to go on a snack run.

———

We finally make it back from the Shoppette, faces flushed, clutching snacks.

"Dude, I don't think we should hang out in the barracks," Nicole pants, and I know she's right.

"Yeah, but, where? I'm not driving anywhere."

"Well duh, neither am I. Hmm." Her eyes wander, then land on the side of the road. "Oh, hey! How about the PLF blocks?"

The three-foot-high, five-foot-long cement blocks across from the barracks are set up for the riggers and Rangers to practice their parachute landing falls. Nicole and I jump off of them like kindergarteners at recess, giggling hysterically. When we get tired of that, the blocks make a perfect place to lie down and gaze up at where the stars would be visible, if not for all the base's light pollution. Unlike my first mushroom experience, this trip makes me feel carefree and relaxed. It almost allows me to forget I'm not only on a military post, but actually … a soldier? Wait—how the hell did that happen? Lying on the prickly cement, I feel my mind whirring, as though it's kicking into gear for the first time. The reality of the life I've chosen is beginning to set in.

I wanted to be a journalist, so to set myself along that path, I had done two semesters at community college and then … enlisted in the military? True, the occupational specialty I'd selected required learning the basic skills of journalism, but beyond that, the similarities ended. It occurs to me that if I'd tried psychedelic drugs before the Army recruiter had called my house, the odds that I'd decide to take him up on his offer might've been significantly slimmer.

A year and a half ago I was sitting with a roomful of other potential recruits in downtown Syracuse at the military entry processing station, while stern men in uniform ordered us to fill out every answer on the questionnaire, especially those having to do with drugs. We'd all nudged and winked at each other, knowing we planned to do as our recruiters had instructed and check *No* for every single box that asked about drugs, no matter what the actual answer might be—these questionnaires were just documentation of lies the military wanted the rest of the nation to believe.

"Whatever you do, check *No*," we'd all reminded each other before loading up the van to MEPS that day. "Especially if the answer is *Yes*." Any admitted drug use was liable to get us initially disqualified, but for psychedelics, you couldn't even get a waiver. In spite of a tendency toward recklessly experimenting with everything unknown, I hadn't used any substances of that kind, and I didn't take the time to find out what was the big problem.

Now, flat on my back on the PLF block, watching reality repeatedly disappear and reappear, I'm beginning to understand. Who would want the task of indoctrinating someone whose mind has already had a taste of its own limitlessness?

But it's too late: I've already been indoctrinated. As much as I want to think I've resisted it, even under the influence of strong drugs I still feel loyal to the team and the mission, although I don't understand the point of the mission and have only the bare minimum of faith remaining in my team. Ever since members of our division bombed and invaded Iraq a few months ago, the main mission of the public affairs soldiers like me, who didn't deploy with them, is to create daringly bland human-interest pieces about the on-post goings-on. It's our job to "tell the Army Story" of the war to the soldiers in a way that'll keep everyone wanting to fight it. It feels like selling burgers to cows while their families are fattened for slaughter.

I don't know enough about the military, the government, U.S. and world history, or my own nation's foreign policy to understand exactly why every civilian news article I read insists that the invasion and occupation of Iraq is a terrible, horrible, no-good, very-bad idea. I do know I have to do my work and stay out of trouble long enough to get the job training and college money my recruiter promised, and keep focused on my day-to-day duties. For someone who wanted to be a war reporter, I've given an embarrassingly small amount of thought to whatever the hell is the deal with the war to which I'm going to be eventually deployed. My attention has been much more sharply focused on my other object of mandated loyalty—the team. The other soldiers in the PA team mostly resent me, and I hate to admit I can't blame them. I'm brand-new to the unit and I've been assigned to a post that everyone else desperately wanted—naturally I've become the black sheep of our dysfunctional public affairs family. I'm usually able to nudge the tension into my subconscious, but it doesn't make my job any easier.

Still flat on my back in the thick evening haze, the idea that this is all a crazy game floats to the surface of my mind and hovers there. We soldiers are all in the game together, giving up our freedom to the government for education, money, job opportunities, life purpose, or whatever else lured us into the uniform. We were all sucked in, chewed up, and swallowed into the belly of the beast, where we'll be digested for X number of years before whatever the military can't use is shat out the other end, dead or alive. We've been given a mission, but that's only an important-sounding word for a job. Its noble purpose, as far as I can tell from my lowly position, is to create a profit for the people running the business—the business, in this case, being war.

Stretched out on the PLF blocks, all of it seems so far away, small, and meaningless. I feel free of all the restrictions and definitions that have been forced on me since my first day of this definitively non-sane let's-be-a-soldier adventure. My public affairs team seems tiny and silly. The mission, whatever it really is, slips out of my mind entirely. For a few hours, I'm just a human being lying on a block of concrete under the night sky, laughing about everything and nothing with another human being.

My surroundings become familiar again as the drugs wear off. Am I really lying out in the open like this? What if someone walks by? Fuck, what if someone I know walks by? Paranoia creeps in, a skulking cat plucking me out of the place where I've been able to see the game for what it is, plopping me down into my scared old skin.

As the sky slowly turns from late-night black into a dingy morning gray, words drift into my consciousness: *The military might have my body, but my mind is mine to meddle with.* A wave of relief washes over me. I turn to Nicole.

"We should do this more."

"Fuck yeah, dude."

We make our way back into the barracks. The Beige Mile is empty of life forms, but evidence of their debasement is everywhere: empty beer cans and liquor bottles, cigarette butts, discarded chewing tobacco cans, full spit bottles, single socks, poorly-cleaned vomit. The floor is sticky and the air stinky with the ghosts of many packs of smokes. As we move down the hall past each brown door, we hear passed-out snores intermingled with the squeaks of bed springs groaning under the weight of local drunken-club-bunny bodies being aggressively smashed by horny, angry soldiers. This is my world—but it doesn't have to be my life.

Nicole and I unlock our side-by-side doors.

"Next weekend?" she grins.

"Next weekend."
I sleep soundly.

A CASE OF THE CRUD

It begins with airborne bacteria-ridden dust particles easing their way into every pore and orifice of my defenseless body. It doesn't end until thirty seconds before I have lost my will to live.

Its presence is first signaled by a cough and a sniff, harbingers of respiratory doom which I promptly dismiss as "just a bit of something in the back of my throat." Poor little fool.

The next morning I wake up, brush the dirt off my olive-drab-green cot, roll over, and discover that my verbal output has been reduced to a single syllable: "Guh."

I want to call in sick, but I forfeited that right when I took my oath of enlistment. I am no longer a person, but a number—or, as my superiors regularly refer to me, a body. Uncle Sam doesn't believe in sick days. A monosyllabic whimper escapes my lips. This deployment has hardly started, and it's not even the terrorists taking me down. Or maybe it is. I can't tell anymore.

I struggle into my desert-camouflage uniform and boots. Normally done with hardly a second thought, it's now a task of

Sisyphean proportions, as I am concentrating the majority of my energy on simply breathing continuously with as few interruptions as possible.

IiiiiiinSNORK … oooouuutGURK. I don't want to be a mouth-breather, but a mass of phlegm has staked its claim in my nasal passages and is not going anywhere. I can feel it blocking traffic in my sinuses as I raise the first tissue of the day to my trembling nostrils.

Now it's time to brave the tenacious Kuwaiti dust storm outside my tent. There was no dust until the rain stopped yesterday, but with only tents and sparse temporary structures to block the wind, the drying mud under my feet is now scooped up in gusts and deposited in the creases of my eyelids as I attempt to navigate the still-new terrain. I'm not sure how long our unit will be staying here to prepare for movement, but I can tell the grime of Camp Buehring will be with me long after we've crossed into Iraq.

Wrapping a brown cotton scarf around my nose and mouth and donning oversized, thickly-plastic'd ballistic eyewear, I shove my patrol cap down on my head as far as it will go. We're not authorized, for reasons only known as "orders," to wear the sensible headgear we were issued—the boonie cap that comes with a full brim and strap to hold it on—so I clamp my hand down firmly atop my crown, sling my M16-A2 rifle over my shoulder, and bend slightly forward at the waist. I am now prepared to walk outside.

The January wind whips around me. Each step I take is more pitiful than the one before it. My eyes gush water, sending streams of dust down my cheeks. My nose releases an impressive stream of snot, and as I remove my hand from my head to reach for another tissue, the wind neatly pops my hat off my head and into the air.

It takes a few minutes to catch up with my hat. The wind hasn't blown it far, but my muscles have been weakened by The Crud rapidly permeating my entire body. There is also the matter of my M16, which normally sits, lightly dormant, on my back, but now seems to be ball-and-chaining me to the ground.

I execute a pathetic stumble for a half-mile down the dirt road to the camp's dining facility and make a valiant attempt at eating breakfast. Without the ability to breathe through my nose, polite chewing is impossible. Instead I chomp away at my cereal in a bovine daze, barely aware of my fellow soldiers inching slowly away. I have nearly emptied my first package of tissues, and my head is feeling denser every second. In fifteen minutes, I have to report for duty.

My work day is a blur of half-consciously-composed morale articles about our division's highly-successful training in Kuwait, and my night is a relentless struggle to breathe through at least one nostril. In the morning I go to sick call. I wait wretchedly in line for an hour behind a herd of my fellow soldiers, all of whom are suffering from some Crud variation, or are on crutches, or are trying to convince the medics that they have malaria and need to be sent home. The medics give each of us a pill bottle full of 800-milligram Motrin. They tell me not to come back unless my eyes start bleeding. "It's just the Crud."

Over the next several days, I go through enough Kleenex to carpet the Vatican. My brain's functions dwindle slowly until my actions are limited to lurching around at a slow shuffle and mumbling profanities between shallow breaths. I still report for duty every day—a head cold, no matter how severe, is not considered just cause for a day of rest. This being the case, my entire unit contracts the Crud, passing it back and forth freely like a germ-infested Frisbee.

When it has finally run its course, I am exhausted. My nostrils are raw, my skin is blotchy, my eyes are swollen and my throat is hoarse. I take the first deep breath through my nose in days and exhale slowly, cautiously.

Could it be? I ask myself. Have I ... recovered?

I have indeed recovered. In fact, I have recovered just in time to put on all of my gear, body armor and helmet included, pack up my bags, and climb aboard a C-130 with several dozen of my comrades-in-arms. My training in Kuwait is complete, and now I am headed for Iraq, where I will spend the next eleven (or more!) months.

The soldier sitting next to me coughs, then sniffs. Nobody bats an eyelash. We all know that if any of the higher-ups cared about our health, they wouldn't be so quick to send us to war.

It's going to be a long deployment.

THE TWIG THAT BROKE THE CAMEL'S BACK

Three years in the Army have confirmed my belief that all authority figures will eventually be inspired to resent me. It's not a revelation—one of my parents' favorite pastimes was regaling new friends with tales of my unmanageability—and if he'd wanted to, my recruiter could have figured out that I was more inclined to question orders than follow them. But I enlisted during a time of deep need for warm bodies, and my glaring flaws were overlooked. I knew before the end of Basic Training that the armed forces and I were a terrible fit for each other, but even then, it was already too late. I've signed on the dotted line, raised my right hand, and taken an oath to "protect and defend the Constitution against all foes both foreign and domestic." Now, the only ways to quit are punishable by prison time.

After the first few weeks in Baghdad, my patience has already been worn as thin as our aging commanding general's hair. On the rare occasions I'm sent off the base to do any reporting, I'm constrained by the requirement to pretend I don't see all the destruction our invasion seems to be leaving as a legacy—even if I tried to write about the wreckage all around me, my supervisors would never let my words go to print. They're too preoccupied with their own problems to take a risk on content that might draw the commander's attention to them.

My first-line supervisor, Staff Sergeant Smudge, has an ongoing medical issue that keeps her in the clinic and out of the headquarters. That leaves Private First Class Twig and me as the sole peons of Master Sergeant Bradley, a career public affairs soldier who, like the rest of our team, is on his first-ever deployment. It's his job to please the lieutenant colonel, and he shows it by exuding a contagious degree of anxiety at all times. He took over as our team's top enlisted leader not long before we left the States, and the task overwhelmed him immediately. Now, despite his friendly face, he rarely makes eye contact. He has a knack for repelling human interaction by hunching over his desk whenever possible, typing furiously away at what he wants us all to assume is work. He makes it clear in every possible way that he has no time for anything, up to and including training Twig.

It's not that my co-worker has never been taught to do his job—the training has just somehow resisted taking hold in his brain. Under different circumstances, he might have been required to repeat his course at our Orwellian alma mater, the Defense Information School, but the Army needs public affairs soldiers, and Twig's glaring shortcomings in the areas of writing, photography, newspaper layout, and reporting were duly overlooked by his instructors. He arrived at our division, his first permanent-duty assignment, with an empty toolkit, and I remain convinced the only reason the rest of us didn't chase him out of town with sharp sticks was because we didn't have enough time or energy left after redoing all of his work.

Our deployment began in January, and by April, Staff Sergeant Smudge is on intermittent bed rest, rarely making a personal appearance in the headquarters. Master Sergeant Bradley is firmly entrenched up the colonel's ass. There's one person left to train Twig, and that person feels the job to be far beyond their pay grade. I am a mere Specialist, after all—just one inconsequential rank above his. My position of authority is not mandated but implied, and we both know it. On one of her unexpected days in the office, I appeal to a higher authority.

"Sergeant Smudge, can we talk?"

"What's up, Specialist?"

"It's Twig."

"What about him?"

"Mainly? He's useless."

Before our division shipped off to Iraq, I'd already been stationed with our public affairs section for two years, and Sergeant Smudge and I were as close to friends as a junior-enlisted and noncommissioned officer could be. Now, I have a sinking feeling we might destroy each other before the terrorists can. Twig is the only soldier left to help me design and edit the bi-weekly task force newspaper, and my temper-moderation skills are just about on par with his technical and creative skills: hovering slightly above nonexistent.

"Sergeant Smudge." She swivels slowly in her chair, turning toward me to reveal an exquisitely annoyed expression. I choke back an involuntary gulp. "We really need to talk."

She sighs, eyes orbiting their sockets. Her loose blonde bun bobs beneath her collar, then back above it, occupying a space that mysteriously manages to exist both outside and within regulation. If I wasn't so annoyed with her, I'd be impressed.

Sergeant Smudge's tone defies me to state my purpose. "Come on, Specialist. What did he do wrong now? I'm late for my appointment."

"We could save time if I told you everything he did right this week."

"Don't be mean. It's not like he's doing anything *that* wrong."

She has a point. Our division is constantly under fire in the media for much larger mistakes than typos and shoddy internal-newspaper design. The generals are more concerned with keeping embedded press away from the action than with keeping their "command information" free of misprints. Even on the base, there have been slips—one soldier was actually quoted as saying he felt like cannon fodder, "Out here sweeping the sidewalks," while rockets and mortars dropped in. But my job is to make a decent newspaper, and having spent the past two years working with soldiers who hold passionate opinions about the Oxford comma, I've come to take it seriously. The option of apathy has never even been on the table before. Now, I'm expected to accept that it's the only one left.

The occupation of Iraq ("reconstruction," as we've repeatedly been told to call it) is slinking into its third year, and I'm fighting my own, equally futile war in the task force headquarters. I didn't set out to be such a stickler for a job I know in my heart to be pointless at best and deceptive at worst, but my inner overachiever (admittedly less vocal than my outer underachiever) is something of a perfectionist whether I like it or not, and just won't leave me alone. I can't throw up my hands and settle for sloppily thrown-together propaganda—not even for the sake of team unity.

Nobody even reads the stupid newspaper, I tell myself, knowing that even if it went straight from my hard drive into the burn-box, I would care whether the commander's chosen news was laid out right. When I'm the soldier tasked with burning "classified" documents at the end of the day, I watch my work go up in the most literal smoke available, unable to convince my supervisor that this is a pointless task ("But why would we burn them when we just mailed boxes of them all over the country?" "Well, um, because we do?") and later that afternoon, I still find myself unable to overlook a misplaced comma. Every time I'm on the verge of finally giving up my goal of flawless pseudo-journalism in favor of harmonious mediocrity, Twig hands me more of his work to edit. And as my eyes float first over all the obvious errors, and then the less-obvious ones, and then the ones so subtle I would swear he made them on purpose, I forget that none of it matters. I feel defeated. I sit at my desk and stare at the wall which I imagine might, in a civilian workplace, contain a window.

Upon entering the uninterrupted walls of the building where we spend at least eighty-four hours each week, we are all greeted daily by a stark non-design scheme, like the kind of mental institutions that gently ease patients away from stability. The hulking monstrosity has a massive footprint, like a Costco with heavily-armed guards and no snack bar. Its exterior is a matte mustard that nearly matches the dust coating every exposed surface. To make up for allowing in zero watts of natural light, its interior is bathed in a fluorescent glow twenty-four hours a day by way of ceiling-tile lights that emit a charming perpetual buzz for ambiance. The generals and other brass are ensconced in cheerless offices constructed with particle board that perimeter a wide-open floor plan with high ceilings and a conspicuous lack of permanent walls. There is a constant din: phones, radios, loudspeaker announcements, voices that hush only in the middle of the night and, sometimes, during rocket attacks.

Nearly every inch of floor space is partitioned into tan cubicles of varying heights, with each section of operations assigned roughly half the square-footage needed for soldiers to avoid breathing directly into each other's mouths. Soldiers who work the day shift are within elbowing distance of at least one other human at all times, while those on the night shift get the luxury of personal space as an incidental perk for spending the majority of their waking hours in a world without sunlight.

After a couple of months working within a two-foot radius of Twig, I'm daydreaming about the night shift, even though switching shifts would mean giving up my long-held hopes of becoming something like the war reporter that my recruiter, with a straight face, had promised I would be. On night shift, instead of going more frequently outside the relatively secure walls of our forward operating base to report on the Army's side of the war, I'd be resigning myself to a permanent desk job, an idea I loathe. But working from 8:30 p.m. to 8:30 a.m. would remove Twig from my daily life so I can do my work in peace, unhindered by my fear of accidentally throat-chopping him while blacked out in a rage over his dozenth illegible paragraph. I'm already stuck making a newspaper instead of covering news. If I had to come all the way to Baghdad to do a job I could've done anywhere with electrical outlets and internet access, I want, at a bare minimum, to be able to do that job without his heavy-breathing presence right next to me, hijacking my limited attention with inane commentary as I rewrite his articles and redesign his pages.

"I got into an argument with this guy over email."

"Oh?"

"Yeah. And I sent him the perfect insult response."

"Good for you."

"But he didn't reply."

"That's too bad."

"Then I checked my email and guess what?"

"No."

"I sent it to myself instead of him."

"Of course you did."

Pause.

"Damn ... I've never emailed *myself* an insult before."

"Please stop talking."

I finally put in my request to change shifts. My remaining sanity is at stake. There are still nine months to go in this deployment. If the situation doesn't change, I fear I'll lose the ability to keep my shit together, and instead spew it all over Twig—or worse, someone with the authority to ruin my life. If I can't quit this job that doesn't seem to have any real value to humanity, I want to be able to do it the right way the first time, without being bothered. I have clearly forgotten which Army I'm in.

———

I've been close to my boiling point for weeks when Staff Sergeant Smudge approaches, her face cloaked in an illegible expression. "We need to talk."

Could this be about how she's finally going to train Twig? I'm low on sleep, high on aggravation and adrenaline, and even higher on Rip-Its, those little caffeinated cans of sugar-drink that we all grab six-at-a-time from the dining facility. A few months ago, I anticipated a year as a war reporter in a combat zone. Sure, I'd only be able to write what I was told, but I assured myself this was just practice for the *real* reporting I'd do one day as a civilian. Now, I feel defeated, rotting away in a combat-zone cubicle, waiting—wishing—for one of those incessant mortar attacks to successfully explode the headquarters.

I follow Staff Sergeant Smudge outside to the smoking area, a narrow strip of benches to the left and right of the main entrance between the headquarters doors and the guard shack. As usual, it's packed with soldiers taking our only form of permissible break from work. A few of my friends approach, then back quickly away when they see Staff Sergeant Smudge and surmise that this time I'm not out here for a smoke.

She stops when we're still a few yards away from them and turns to face me. "Stand at parade-rest." *Ah, this personality today. Weren't we friends yesterday?* I comply, locking my hands behind my back with pointed stiffness. "I know you've been complaining to soldiers from other sections about your shift, and I want you to stop it."

"Excuse me, Sergeant?"

"You heard me."

Visions of the past months' madness dancing in my head, I stare at her blankly for a moment. Exhaustion and irritation combine and combust and with my next breath, I'm doing the one thing to Staff Sergeant Smudge that you're never supposed to do to a noncommissioned officer: saying exactly what I think. The words pour from my mouth in a freely-flowing stream of unfiltered indignation, with expletive-laced tributaries all rushing together to form one mighty river of desperate profanity. When I stop for breath, Staff Sergeant Smudge blinks.

"I'm the one giving *you* the counseling here!" she sputters. Three minutes later, we're in Master Sergeant Bradley's office watching his head whip back and forth between us. Staff Sergeant Smudge explains the situation through gritted teeth as I helpfully shake with rage beside her. Master Sergeant Bradley's face is the exact opposite of pleased.

Insubordination carries serious consequences. Most soldiers, when confronted by not just one, but two higher-ranking noncommissioned officers, will choose to express no opinion other than "Roger, Sergeant." On even the least painful days I struggle with keeping my thoughts inside my head, but now I've fallen off the end of my rope and am plummeting to certain doom. My last sliver of hope for the future has left the windowless building, taking with it my last hint of ability to keep the present from falling apart. I want to turn my brain off and play the game, but as hard as I try, I'm unable to quit caring about both the purpose of my work *and* its quality.

The stark walls of the headquarters close in on me. I hear myself protesting the hypocrisy, the injustice, the everything-wrong, but there's nothing I can say to breach the wall of authority standing impenetrably before me. Master Sergeant Bradley is raising his voice now. *He never raises his voice. I should probably be afraid.* But there's no room for fear—the lunacy of the whole situation has flooded all my senses. My head is spinning. Large, unsoldierly tears are streaming down my cheeks. In a brief moment of lucidity, I find myself praying to a God I no longer think I believe in, for a mortar to fall on the headquarters and put us all out of our misery. *Did I say that out loud?* Major parts of my brain seem to have shut down entirely. By the time Master Sergeant Bradley stops speaking and it's my turn to respond, I hear myself glaringly inform him that I plan to bring this issue to our company commander—technically the correct protocol, but clearly not the right answer.

The two bewildered NCOs stare at me. They open their mouths. They close them again. They give me the rest of the day off "to decompress." I can't blame them—I don't want to be around me when I'm like this either.

———

Thanks to a bout of cosmic timing, another unit needs a public affairs soldier for a few days, so my bosses send me to Forward Operating Base Prosperity, in the part of inner Baghdad dubbed the International Zone—casually known as the IZ or Green Zone. I cover joint U.S.-Iraqi Army patrols and a night raid, giddy over the chance to finally do some form of reporting. The articles I write make no mention of the constant desertion of the hastily-assembled Iraqi security forces, or of the intelligence leak that botched the raid. I'm still not sure what form of reporting this technically is, but I do know I would rather risk my life in the streets and landfills of Baghdad than spend my days in a military-issue cubicle, seven thousand miles from home.

On the fourth morning at FOB Prosperity, I wake up with a fever of 103, accompanied by shivers, shakes, body aches, and a sore throat. I can't swallow food. A bomb has just gone off nearby, and the medics, annoyed that I'm bothering them with a non-combat-related injury, dismiss me with the terse explanation that they don't know what the problem is. The next morning, the problem has created a massive lump on the side of my neck. I name the lump "Rufus." On the sixth day, barely functioning, I manage to heave my body armor over my shoulders and maneuver the straps of my Kevlar helmet around Rufus long enough to board a Blackhawk helicopter back to Camp Liberty, where the medics pump me full of antibiotics and go out for a smoke.

"We don't know why you're sick, but this will probably help," they assure me when they come back in. "We think it will, anyway." I'm not sure I believe them, but after nearly three days of examining what they decide to call a *peritonsillar abscess* (the technical term for "lump on the side of the neck," I groaningly deduce), I'm not allowed to turn down treatment. The antibiotics manage to rid me of Rufus and the whole ordeal gets me another couple of days away from the desk I share with Twig.

When I get back to the headquarters, still sickly but out of allotted recovery days, I find Twig has proudly put together the sloppiest-looking newspaper my aching eyes have ever seen. No one else seems to notice or care. I notice and care extra on their behalf.

"Twig. What even *is* this? It looks like you laid out these pages with your eyes almost fully closed. And I can't look at a single story without seeing typos and syntax errors, like, everywhere."

"Come on, I think it looks fine."

"Yeah, I'm sure you do."

———

My throat is still sore from the remainders of Rufus but I smoke two cigarettes anyway, extending my break as long as I possibly can. One of my buddies from another section of the headquarters, Sergeant Hellman, comes out to join me. He's perpetually bitter, a side effect of having his military occupational specialty abruptly switched from "combat engineer" to "the command sergeant major's driver."

"Dude!" He grins, a cigarette sticking out of his mouth's left crease. "You're back! How was the Green Zone?"

"It was all right. Amazing, compared to working in this fucking place."

"Even with Sergeant Smudge gone?"

"Yeah ... Twig's still here."

"Oh yeah, that guy. I saw him getting bitched out by the sergeant major the other day. He was wearing his patrol cap crooked or something."

"Yep, sounds like him."

"How'd he fuck with you this time?"

"Oh my fucking lord. He's just the biggest pain my ass ever had. Did you see the newspaper this week?"

"Yeah, why?"

"He put it together while I was gone. It looks like shit."

"Really?"

"Yeah, it looks like a drunk child produced it."

"I mean … I couldn't tell."

"Well … I can tell."

"So? Nobody else can. Who fuckin' cares?"

"I do! I've been doing this job for almost three years, and my name is on the masthead as the associate editor, and I want the paper to look like somebody put it together on purpose."

"Uh … what's a masthead?"

"Goddammit. Never mind. I have to get back inside."

"All right. Don't worry about those fuckers, they're all ass-kissing dumbasses anyway. Just keep your head down. Eight more months to go."

"Yeah, yeah, yeah. See you later."

—

I spend my time off brainstorming ways to get kicked out of the Army without losing my benefits or ending up in jail.

"You could get pregnant," my friend Suzanne suggests. She has kids of her own back home.

"That's its own jail," I retort despondently. "At least with the Army there's a *chance* of it being over eventually." We're sitting on the splintering wooden steps of the rickety porch affixed to the trailer where we live in side-by-side thin-walled rooms. The temperature is pushing 100 degrees at eight a.m. The metal band on her lighter, sitting only a few minutes in the sun, burns my thumb as I light a cigarette and hand her the pack. She pulls one out and lights it, taking a distracted drag.

"The Army is kind of like a baby that never grows up. Like, it just sucks at your teat till you fall over."

"They should definitely make you a recruiter."

"Dude, they should! I love this shit!"

"Uh, are you sure you're listening to yourself?"

"Yeah, yeah. It sucks, but I still love it."

"You're really selling it."

"I mean, deployment is like that. But other than this, I only have to do a weekend a month and two weeks of annual training. I don't know how you active-duty guys do this all the time."

"It's like a vampire that kills you, then brings you back to life and kills you again. Every day." Like being a cog in a machine that hates you, I once heard someone say.

She nods thoughtfully. "How much longer do you have to be in?"

"Two years."

"Mmm-hmm. Yeah." She smashed her cigarette into the butt can balancing precariously on the porch railing. "Good luck, dude. You'll be fine."

"Thanks, buddy. Need another smoke for later?"

"Yeah, I'll get ya back."

I'm in a war zone, with no guarantee of tomorrow on any given day, and my stamina is being tested not by terrorists, but by my own team. I can't quit the Army without a fight, and the last thing I want is to be removed from my job after all the work I've put in to get to this point. All I can see is that the only way to rid myself of the dual curse of Twig's incompetence and my leaders' lack of desire to lead is to change shifts.

I put in weeks of requesting and cajoling, but the stone faces of my NCOs deflect every attempt. Grimly accepting my fate, I devote all of my focus to my work until I can escape for two weeks of mid-tour leave. On my return to Baghdad, I get the news I've been waiting for: in three days, I'll be moved to night shift. To my thrilled disbelief, it looks like I'm getting what I want.

———

"You wanted to see me, Sergeant Bradley?"

"Yes, sit down. Since you're starting a new shift, I need to give you an initial counseling session."

"Okay."

"All right, um, let's start. Here's a list of your new job responsibilities."

"Wait, new job responsibilities? You mean in addition to the newspaper?"

"Ah, no. Instead of the newspaper."

"But I'm the associate editor."

"Well, that's the thing. You're not going to be the associate editor anymore."

"But … why … who …?"

"Twig is going to take over as associate editor."

"Sergeant, are you kidding? He can't even edit his own work! I wanted to be moved so I could do my job without him bothering me!"

"All right, I'm going to have to move on to the next part of this counseling. You're being moved to night shift because of your inability to co-exist with co-workers. Your new job is to compile a daily media roundup of articles about the task force and division, formatted for review by the commanding general using the method detailed in this packet."

"It looks like all I'm doing is Googling news articles about Iraq, copying them, pasting them in a Word document, and emailing them to you."

"You're also going to be emailing me some attachments that will be emailed to you every night from Corps. Here's an example."

"That looks like … a compilation of news articles about Iraq. Are those the same articles I'll be copying?"

"Well … kind of. Yours will be formatted differently."

"It looks like the only difference is that the headlines are bold instead of italic."

"Oh? Well, I guess that's the difference, then."

"Isn't that kind of … pointless?"

"I wouldn't call it that, no. Maybe a little redundant, but, heh, that's the Army for you."

"Ha."

"Any other questions?"

"Where do I turn in my two-week notice, Sergeant?"

"Ha, that's funny. Hang on to your sense of humor. Only six more months in Iraq to go, right?"

"Seven months, Sergeant."

"Cheer up, Specialist. It's not so bad. And remember, if you ever need someone to talk to …"

"Yes, Sergeant?"

"Well, there's always the chaplain. Other than that, I guess you're on your own."

"Thanks, Sergeant."

"I'm here to help." He stands up. "Here, you're going to have to sign this counseling statement."

—

Master Sergeant Bradley is gone before the ink on my signature is dry. The fluorescent lights above my head flicker. The din of the headquarters dies down as the day shift filters out and the next shift settles in. The night stretches out before me like a lightless tunnel.

I sink into my chair. *Couldn't just let Twig be, could you? Couldn't just settle for mediocrity like everyone else.* The pounding in my head is drowned out only by the booming of a nearby mortar explosion. As usual, a few seconds too late, I hear the camp's robotic loudspeaker: "Incoming, incoming, incoming!" I close my eyes and chant along like it's an old, familiar song, or some far-off church's pealing bell signaling the start of a dark new day.

FREEDOM REST

If you ever suspect you have a strong personal moral code, here's how to know for sure: devote a hefty chunk of your time and energy to the production of morale-boosting half-truths about a war in which you and your friends are currently endangered. If, when bending that moral code into complex knots in an effort to keep your personal self out of trouble and appease your superiors, you feel remotely guilty about it ... congratulations! There's still a tiny part of you that knows the difference between right and wrong. But don't worry—over time, you'll acquire a special flair for deadening that guilt with copious amounts of alcohol. Even if it's prohibited. *Especially* if it's prohibited. Compared to spinning a questionably-motivated quagmire of a war into an optimistic peace process, sneaking a bottle here or there will feel like the least of your crimes.

I've already spent the better (or worse) part of twelve months in Iraq as part of what I have come to recognize as an illegally-invading force. I have no idea whether I'll make it home alive but then, self-preservation isn't my strongest instinct. Not that keeping soldiers alive seems to be a priority for Commander-in-Chief Bush, or Vice President Dick, or any of the other politicians who sent us all here. Nobody complains except in the way that everyone complains. We know what we signed up for, as our superiors are fond of reminding us, though I'm never sure I believe them. It's not like this is a typical war—we aren't fighting an opposing military. This is the War on Terror. Anyone could be a bad guy. Maybe even us.

When we showed up in Iraq back in January, we were greeted with a multitude of briefings—how to evade enemy capture, how to duck behind concrete barriers in case of incoming mortar fire, how to say "Stop or I'll shoot!" in sounds that resemble Arabic—but no information about when or how our engagement in Baghdad would end. This deployment is supposed to last a year, after which another division will come in and take over. These rotations, we're told, will continue until the mission is accomplished. But Bush already declared the mission accomplished a year and a half ago, standing on an aircraft carrier in a flight suit, and still there is no end to deployment rotations in sight. Most of us lowly enlistees haven't finished college, but it doesn't require a degree to receive a loud and clear message, transmitted via a constant barrage of rocket attacks and improvised roadside bombs: the Iraqis are not liberated, and the war is not won. In light of this development, we on the Task Force Baghdad public affairs team have been directed to refer to the occupation as a "reconstruction."

My title in the reconstruction, "public affairs specialist," could have easily been discarded in favor of the snappier "propagandist." I'm deployed to Baghdad to help collect information and mold it into palatable portions of digestible fact-sausage, mashing carefully-chosen details together to create newsy-looking articles to remind soldiers that we are the good guys, and we are winning. The public affairs team's mission is simple: amplify positive news, downplay or ignore negative news. Conveniently, neither of these tactics can be legally defined as lying. If there is anything remotely victorious to report, we send out a press release, splash it across every military newspaper and TV broadcast, print it on high-gloss card stock, and make it as glaringly ubiquitous as possible. The rest of the time, we are in damage-control mode. The Army calls us journalists.

My new friend Anna and I both enlisted as teenagers. We're now in our early twenties. While friends in our respective home-towns in northern California and upstate New York are finishing college and re-occupying their parents' houses, we have been occu-pying the explosively shocked-and-awed nation of Iraq.

The word "interrogation" has developed a negative connota-tion in the media, so Anna's job description is officially "intel-ligence-gathering." Once she finds out which, if any of the coalition's Iraqi prisoners, have actually committed any crimes, her superior officers can more accurately determine which details of their arrests to conceal. As it turns out, she tells me, few of the people who are dragged in, blindfolded and zip-tied by U.S. troops, hold any major role in resisting our occupation of their country or control of their government. Our public affairs team has been instructed to call them all insurgents.

When I look up the definition of "insurgent," I find the answer—"a rebel or revolutionary"—vague enough to be deemed not-incorrect, and mentally put the matter to rest. We already call prisoners "detainees," the occupation "reconstruction," and the war itself a "peace-keeping mission." The leap from "individual possibly loosely affiliated with various groups who oppose the U.S.-led coalition and its handpicked Iraqi government" to "insurgent" is more like a hop. Maybe even a shuffle.

"If we get blown up here, how do you think your office will spin it?" Anna's voice jerks my attention back to the mission at hand.

"Probably the way we do all the other deaths by stupidity—call it non-combat-related. That's what we do for the huffers." Soldiers have been incessantly warned not to huff Dust-Off, but for some, it's still an all-too tempting crutch in the absence of alcohol. "Same thing for the suicides."

"I guess that's technically true ... oh, shit, we're stopping. This must be the place." The up-armored SUV idles as the driver speaks to us in a low voice, making eye contact through the rear view mirror to avoid turning his head.

"We're going in," he says, tilting his head at the other soldier in the front of the truck. "You two have to stay hidden back there, okay? Otherwise we could all be in deep shit." We nod. "Okay, we'll be right back. What did you want, again?"

"Vodka!" we reply in unison whispers.

"Got it. We'll be quick." They slam the massive armored doors behind them and disappear into the lit-up door of a small shop. I turn to Anna.

"I don't think I've been this nervous about a liquor run since I was underage."

"Oh man, me either. Just stay down."

———

The September sun set over Baghdad an hour or so ago in its usual flamboyant way, with complete disregard to the chaotic city darkening beneath it. Sleek black helicopters owned by aptly-named private security contractor Blackwater buzzed overhead alongside the Apache, Blackhawk, and Chinook helicopters making their obnoxious laps through the sky. We lounged by the pool, tuning them out.

This luxurious haven, now enclosed within concrete barriers, was Saddam Hussein's Republican Guard officers' club not so long ago, complete with clean, spacious rooms and a massive kidney-shaped pool just outside the glass doors of the lower lobby, through ornate arches and columns. Now Saddam has been in jail for two years, and his posh patio hosts U.S. soldiers with cracking skin and uniform-sleeve tans, all dressed in swimsuits or crumpled civilian clothes from the bellies of dusty duffel bags, soldiers who shriek with childlike glee as we leap from fifteen- and thirty-foot high-dives into waters once tread by the Ba'ath regime's upper echelons.

"Freedom Rest, an oasis in the center of the Iraqi capital, helps soldiers escape the stress of life on the front lines of war," reads the description posted on the official Freedom Rest website. "There, they can strip away their body armor, lock up their weapons and enjoy time off without leaving the theater of operations." There's no mention of the compound's prior clientele, but it's clear this place was not built for public use, and we all know there's no money without political clout in Baghdad.

"Dude, I bet Saddam peed in this pool," we'd joked to each other at orientation.

Peeling off my body armor and desert camouflage uniform was like shedding a layer of unwanted skin. After nine months deployed, I've lost fifteen pounds and none of my civvies fit, but there's a tiny, cash-only bazaar run by a few Iraqis. They sell me white short-shorts, a fitted black tank top, a lime-green, thigh-grazing dress decorated with shiny, unnecessary sequins—it's almost enough to make me feel like a girl again. I've gone without any feminine effects beyond a looser-than-average hair bun for so long that the simple act of putting on a dress felt even less familiar than the Iraqis who sold it to me.

Local-nationals, we call the Iraqis when we're being polite. They run bazaars at all the forward operating bases. When they aren't in earshot we just call them all "Hajji"—a word that is only supposed to be used with reverence and in reference to Muslims who've made the Hajj, or pilgrimage, to Mecca. Then we soldiers strode in and slapped it on anyone who looked local. We're all used to each other by now ... at least, according to my estimate, they're used to our money, and we're used to having stuff to buy. I figure handing them American dollars is the least I can do, as a newly guilt-ridden foreign invader. *I'm sorry for occupying your country*, I always add silently as I press my money into their open palms, wondering how much they hate us all under those effusive smiles.

We were ordered to hand over our weapons to be locked up on arrival at the hotel compound and ever since, I've been unable to fully shake the feeling I'm forgetting something—I'm used to carrying my weapon at all times. It's my third limb. But, they locked our rifles away and instructed us to relax. After all, they said, this was Freedom Rest—as though along with the freedom to rest, comes the ability to actually do it. Still, the United States went to the trouble of taking over the place, so I might as well give relaxation my best shot. But there's one crucial ingredient missing, and without it, no hope of any real rest.

"It's too bad we don't have anything to drink," Anna had sighed. We'd learned each other's first names just a few hours ago. After changing out of our uniforms into bikinis, using last names felt comically formal; the syllables hung in the air like a bow tie on a puppy. I nodded my agreement about the alcohol situation. It's already been a long, dry deployment, with three months still left to go.

"I don't know why they can't let us drink here. It's not like we're working, or driving anywhere." We rode here in a convoy from Camp Liberty and were dropped off with no way of safely leaving the grounds. The fancy buildings and pristine pool greying in the twilight were surrounded by towering concrete blast walls. Even if leaving the relative security of the compound was allowed, we had no vehicle but our own feet.

"They treat us like children," I grumbled.

"Right? And we're, like, in a war." The Army hadn't trained the California out of her. "How can I interrogate detainees, but I can't have a beer?"

"Who even knows. I have no idea how drinking could be worse for your health than a job at Abu Ghraib. Goddamn General Order Number One."

We've heard that in the "old" Army (generally understood as the days when drill sergeants were allowed to strike privates, cigarettes came in prepackaged meals, and misogyny was more overt), soldiers had been permitted to drink during deployments while off-duty. But this is the new Army, and the new Army has new general orders to govern soldiers' personal lives while at war. General Order Number One rules out drinking, drugs, and a colorful variety of other sins, like possessing or distributing porn or privately-owned firearms, or entering a mosque if you're not Muslim. Like all rules, this general order has a tendency to be broken with varying degrees of skill.

"Maybe one of these guys has something," Anna's eyes wandered around the pool. "What do you think?"

"I don't really want to ask them any favors." We're two of only four women in a group of dozens of soldiers sent off for a few days of R&R in the middle of a year-long deployment, and it's best to avoid asking anything of any of the men here. Not that we can fault them—considering the reason we're all in Baghdad in the first place, it's no wonder they consider any opportunity for conversation an open invitation to invade and occupy our space. As the sun sank out of sight, I leaned back in my chair and lit a cigarette. "We'll figure it out."

———

Jumping out of the SUV back at the compound, bottle in hand, I realize I feel more tense by the pool than I did in the truck. As I thank our driver, a visiting soldier from a nearby base who was now due back at work, my lips are smiling, but my shoulders are stiff. *Am I really more prepared to die in this pointless war than to take a four-day break from it?*

We decide to mix the booze our new friends helped us acquire with Red Bull from the Freedom Rest dining facility to make it last longer. The summer heat that oppressed us all day is welcome now that the sun has set. We retreat to a dark corner of the poolside patio with newly-concocted cocktails in Gatorade bottles—no ice, or we'll give ourselves away. I can almost convince myself this is a real vacation. The pool area is impressive, after all, and there are those huge high-dives. I jumped off the middle one earlier, a fifteen-foot plunge, but haven't dared the thirty-footer yet. We've been told to stay off it while the platform is being repaired. It's made of concrete, but the astroturf and wooden boards on top have been ripped up. The platform itself is functional, as long as you don't mind stepping in some dirt and watching for nails, but the Freedom Rest staff insist it's off-limits. For thrill-seeking soldiers, that only makes it more alluring, though nobody would dare defy the order in broad daylight. But now, it's dark.

A couple hours' worth of strong Red Bull-vodkas later, Anna and the two self-appointed male "bodyguards" from our unit who've been granted drinks of their own, despite not having joined us for the liquor mission, place loud, boozy bets on who will be first to jump off the high dive. The deep end of the pool is unlit, ensuring that the jumper won't be seen. It also means whoever takes the thirty-foot plunge will be leaping into total darkness.

The vodka blurs the minutes between accepting the challenge and executing it. Now I'm on the edge of the board, squinting down into what may as well be a bottomless abyss. There's still time to turn around, climb down, laugh it off. I glance back down at the blank space below me. A thought emerges from the caffeinated cocktail haze in my brain: "This is a spectacularly bad idea." I jump.

The drop is silent and the water, invisible—until I hit it. I know it's water, but if I'm going by the tactile experience, it might as well be a slab of concrete. Unthinking, I've bent my knees in mid-air, and instead of slicing into the pool toes-first, my thighs meet the surface with a resounding SLAP. The pain finally registers when I pull myself out of the water, suddenly stone-cold sober.

I wrap myself in a towel and examine my already-bruising legs, contemplating for the first time with a clear head just how badly this might have gone. One wrong step, and it could have been my demise categorized by a check in the "non-combat-related" column—as though they aren't all combat-related. As though we came here for fun … for rest … for freedom.

HOW TO FIX
AN ARMY MARRIAGE

The longer I spend in the Army, the more thoroughly I understand where, on the military's grand spectrum of disposability, I actually am, and it's far closer to the cockroach end than I want to be. A year in Iraq showed me that no matter what I'm told to write in the post newspaper, the war has not been won, and even though we're calling it Operation Iraqi Freedom, Iraqis have not been freed from anything but their own autonomy. It occurs to me that I'm no freer than they are—after all, I can't quit this job, no matter how guilty I feel for doing it. Not without jail time or a long stay in Canada, anyway.

Furiously documenting my frustrations for strangers on the internet is the only release I've found that doesn't require liver-threatening quantities of alcohol or the risk of prison or communicable disease, so I cling to a nightly ritual: before bed, I plop myself down in front of my desktop computer and vent like a furnace all over the screens of my readers.

"What are you DOING in there?" My husband complains from the living room. We got married a few months before I deployed, and while I was gone, he moved us to this apartment—still in Savannah, but significantly further from my duty station, and significantly closer to his. I hate this apartment almost as much as I hate that he didn't tell me he'd moved us here, and slightly more than I hate how it's stretched my daily commute by fifteen minutes. This place is ugly. Our first place was beautiful. The walls are beige—the other apartment was white. The carpet here is old and dingy—our other carpet was new. Sure, we have an extra room now, but considering at least half our motivation for matrimony was the housing allowance every married soldier gets, I'd rather spend it on a place that doesn't remind me of the living rooms where my high-school friends and I would sit waiting for our dime bags, on couches covered in stems and seeds. I haven't yet forgiven him for this.

"I'm WRITING," I holler back. "To my FRIENDS."

"You mean to your STRANGERS who might be SERIAL KILLERS?"

"THEY'RE NICER TO ME THAN YOU ARE."

"YOU BETTER NOT ME WRITING ABOUT ME."

"OH I DEFINITELY AM."

Sometimes I'm writing about him. Sometimes, writing for strangers (who might, I begrudgingly admit, be serial killers) is all that's keeping me from entirely losing my sense of humor and/or sanity. Presenting my life as a series of performed installments allows me to pretend it's happening to a character I've created, whose plot I can watch unfurl in a graceful arc, from a safe distance, and remain unscathed:

April 25, 2006

Husband and I started our Let's Try To Fix Everything In Three Days Army marriage counseling class today, and believe me when I tell you it was more entertaining than drunk jugglers. There were a couple moments where I was venturing dangerously near to pants-peeing territory, thanks to uncontrollable laughter at each others' expense. The best part was the older man who led our first class, which was about Stress Management. I just thought he was a normal kind of weird until Husband leaned over to me and whispered, "Hey, doesn't he look just like Dave Chappelle, in those skits where he dresses up like an old dude?"

And ... yes. Yes, he did. He actually sounded like him as well. And it is a little bit hard to take someone seriously when you are picturing him saying, "What is ... a badonkadonk?"

Then we got to listen to other couples' marital problems. There was the guy who swore the stove in his house was "broken" ("The cooking. Just. Stopped"). There was the woman who tended to get in fights ("This lady cut me off, and then she got out of her car and started yelling at me. So I beat her ass."). And then of course, there was the Woman Who Just Sits There And Glares.

It was surprisingly not a terrible day. I didn't have to go to work, and that is always a plus. Also, I got to make fun of people in my mind. Obviously, I'm looking forward to going back tomorrow.

Sitting with five other angry couples, in a room decorated with wholesome signage full of helpful suggestions, like how to avoid the temptation to shake one's baby, I feel every bone in my body wishing this hell could be as entertaining in real life as I've somehow managed to make it for strangers on the internet. I can't help silently berating myself for ending up here. *How many more red flags did you need, Self?*

My mind drifts helplessly back to 2003. What was it about him that sucked me in? His warped sense of humor? Was it that he was clearly more intelligent than the average soldier? Either way, once he got my attention, he kept it. His eyes were deep brown. "That's because I'm full of shit," he'd joked. At least, I let myself think he was joking.

We spent the better part of two years getting to know one another via the traditional method of getting drunk in our shared barracks with mutual friends, sleeping together on random weekends, and complaining about people we both didn't like. He may have been showing some signs of violent alcoholism and I may have been neglecting some significant codependency issues, but who were we to let that stand in the way of a budding friends-with-benefitship?

One Saturday night, we went out to our favorite dive bar. Sunday afternoon I woke up hungover, a foggy scene drifting through my brain from the night before. I blinked and rolled over on my side to ease the pressure in my head, dimly aware that there was something I should be remembering.

The lights had been swirling in the bar. Someone was singing karaoke—two people, in an off-key duet. We were laughing at them together. He'd picked me up and swung me around. We'd come back to his recently-roommateless room, giggling, sloppily falling through the door. The building was eerily quiet—they'd been moving people out to the new barracks gradually. Few still remained on the formerly-filled first floor. We felt like we had the whole dilapidated place to ourselves—even the nicotine-stained concrete walls, rotting ceiling tiles, glaring fluorescent lighting, and liquor-sticky floors couldn't dampen our drunken romance.

He'd gazed glossily into my eyes, wobbled, stabilized himself, and kissed me. Then he'd pulled back and said—

"Hey!" I nudged him as he yawned and rubbed his eyes. "Do you remember last night?"

"What about it?"

"There was something you said … right before we went to sleep."

"You mean … when I asked you to marry me?"

It really had happened. I nodded.

"Yeah, I remember. You told me to ask you again in the morning."

I nodded again, slowly. "So …"

"So do you want to get married or what?"

Was I awake? Too many times to count, he'd declared he never wanted to get married. Aside from that, we'd spent more of the last two dozen months at odds with one another than any other dysfunctional quasi-couple I knew. Still, though … "I mean, we do love each other."

"And we both want the housing allowance."

I did love him. At least, I kind of thought I did. And we did both want the extra multi-hundred dollars that all married soldiers were eligible to receive on top of their regular pay. After two years in moldy, decrepit barracks, that stipend would be a golden ticket to independent living.

I smiled. "Let's do it."

———

Everyone had the same response when I announced our engagement: "Really? Are you sure?"

Of course I was sure, I said. We were in love. "But haven't you been complaining about him being a dick for the last year?" Well, yes. But things were different now. We were twenty-one now—more mature. "Ahhm ... okay," they said. "Congratu ... lations."

We got married at the post chapel two months after his drunken proposal, hoping to move into our new apartment as quickly as possible. My parents, who'd attempted to bring me up to be a Good Christian Girl™, were visibly skeptical. The night before the big day, as friends and family milled around the buffet-style restaurant where we'd held our rehearsal dinner, my dad pulled me aside and told me he approved of my choice. I breathed a relieved sigh as he agreed to foot the few bills we had incurred in our hasty, low-budget wedding.

"After all," he said, a wide smile masking his suddenly serious tone, "my daughter will only get married *once*." I emitted what I hoped was a lighthearted chuckle, aggressively crushing any sign of fear that this could all be a terrible mistake.

My new husband and I held our reception in the cheaper room of the shabby officers' club down the road from the Hunter Army Airfield chapel. His buddies fed each of us the same number of cheap whiskey shots, and subsequently delivered us to our wedding-night accommodations in an inebriated haze. In the morning, we began our marriage the same way we began our engagement: with debilitating hangovers.

A month or two in, the novelty of living far from the barracks melted away to reveal our unavoidable incompatibility. I was particularly sensitive (for a soldier). He was particularly aggressive (for a soldier). I was a social drinker. He was a daily drinker. I was an empath. He was a sociopath. The only characteristics we shared were a warped sense of humor, an affinity for intoxicants, and the opinion that the Army was both led and populated by idiots. We failed to count ourselves in that population.

Many individuals, even those possessing a generous dash of masochism, would have cut and run from the marriage before the wedding invitations were sent out. I am not one of those individuals. I am a soldier, dammit—trained to endure even the most unnecessarily painful situations—and not remotely ready to stick a fork in this relationship and call it done. Even if I had been, neither of us wanted to go back to living in the barracks. By the time I was sent to Iraq, we'd sampled nearly every category of domestic conflict, and we were more than ready for a break from one another. We'd been married for four months. In desperate need of a vent for my frustrations, I started the blog.

April 26 –

It should be noted that when you put several dysfunctional couples in a room with one moderator who is encouraging them to 'talk about what makes you angry,' the ensuing conversation will be a whole pile of passive-aggressive fun.

Today was Anger Management Day in our marriage class, which meant we got to go around the room and talk about our spouses and the things they do to make us want to throw them off of tall buildings. In order to communicate our points better, we were each given a piece of paper and some crayons (Yes, crayons. Yes, we are soldiers) and told to draw one scenario in which we became angry. I forgot to take my camera with me, so I do not have a visual representation of Husband's drawing to show you. I will say, however, that it included me, a tiny fairy, and the words, "I like to listen to gay music!"—all elements of an artistic masterpiece.

Although the drawing, in and of itself, was undeniably therapeutic—I drew Husband in red, with a giant gut and tiny calves—my favorite part was when everyone else showed their pictures. One woman drew a picture of two people.

"This," she pointed to a stick figure standing in a kitchen, 'is me last night, cooking chicken, beans and mashed potatoes for my husband for dinner. This [pointing to the other stick figure] is my husband, bringing home Chinese take-out." A chorus of "Oh no he didn't!" and "I hope you didn't give him no chicken!" filled the room. (For the record: she gave him no chicken.)

One of the men drew the side of his own face with a massive hand covering it from the jaw to just above the eyebrow. His wife's hand. "That's what makes me mad." His wife, across the table, smirked.

Another woman held up her drawing. "Here's my three kids, and here's me trying to get them ready for school in the morning. And here is my husband, laying on the bed and watching TV, holding the remote, asking me if I'm ready to go yet."

There were many more fabulous drawings and stories ("and here's my cell phone after he threw it out into the

*road and it got run over") and a good time was had
by all. If we can still laugh at our peers together, there
may be hope for us yet.*

By the second day of Army marriage workshopping, the character I've created is aware that this process is a joke at best, but
my real-life self has fully warmed to the idea that an Army marriage can be successfully workshopped in three days—even *this*
Army marriage. After all, we hardly had any time to settle into
married life before I went to Iraq. It makes sense that we'd hit
some bumps in the road.

After a year-long deployment, nobody who knows either my
husband or I was surprised that my absence did not make our
hearts grow fonder. As the months in Baghdad had dragged on, I
found myself checking every box on the list of things older soldiers
warn younger soldiers their spouses will do during deployment:
Spending money irresponsibly—check. Serial cheating—check.
Buying a shiny new Mustang instead of paying bills, moving to
the new apartment (a creative addition to the list, I can tell by
the low whistles of surprise from my buddies)—check and check.
Lying about all of the above—emphatic check.

After every new revelation, I'd taken stock of the situation:
Did he do something bad? Yes. *Like, unforgivably bad?* Maybe.
Should I leave him? Possibly. Probably. Certainly. *Am I going
to actually leave him?* Well, it's better not to make big decisions
during a deployment, so ... *For real, am I going to leave him?* He
does have all my stuff. *That's a terrible reason to stay.* But what
if he sells everything while I'm gone? *It's still almost definitely a
good idea to break up.* To complement my inner monologue, I'd
poured all my internal conflict into my anonymous online journal,
and every time I made an excuse for my husband's behavior, my
readers would remind me that this situation was not acceptable.

Still, though ... how can I leave him while I'm in Iraq? Aren't we already technically separated?

Three weeks before Christmas, I'd discovered he'd acquired a girlfriend. In September.

He didn't answer the phone when I called. I took my rage to the strangers on the internet.

"LEAVE HIM NOW," they said in unison. After eleven months of hoping, or maybe pretending, everything was going to be fine, I'd finally considered it.

What would a deployment divorce even entail? How could I leave someone who was already seven thousand miles away? What if he took off with all my stuff? Did this mean I'd have to say goodbye to not only my precious housing allowance, but also the additional hundred and fifty dollars per month I was receiving in combat separation pay? And, holy shit, didn't he have my power of attorney?

The power of attorney, at least, I could take care of from Baghdad. I'd done so in a hurry. I was one of the lucky ones. Plenty of soldiers find out about "Jody"—the ubiquitous nickname for the person who takes advantage of our absence by way of taking advantage of our spouses—after all the bank accounts have been drained. My funds were intact, even if my heart and ego were shattered. I could still rebuild my life without him. Right?

My return date approached. Panic set in. Was I really prepared to go "home" to nowhere and nobody? Of course I wasn't. Not even a little bit. Not in this mental state. After all, even if my husband was unfaithful, he was still my husband. For nearly a year I'd missed him, worried that while I was gone he'd run off with a stripper. Now my worst fears had come true—not necessarily the stripper part (although there had been rumors), but that I'd left for war *with* someone and now, like so many soldiers before me, I would be returning to ... no one. I'd been in the Army long enough to expect life to change on a dime, but being suddenly alone was unfamiliar territory. It was easier to be under constant rocket and mortar fire among a thousand other miserable soldiers than to imagine stepping off the plane into a half-emptied apartment.

To the military, I know I'm nothing but a body with convenient access to a mostly-functional brain. I know my value is only as high as my rank (or, if we're being generous, my usefulness). I know my life is expendable. All soldiers wear that knowledge as an invisible blindfold that shields us from seeing our own inherent worth. If we didn't, we'd never be willing to risk death on command. But now, even my husband saw me as expendable—I couldn't help but take it personally.

Retreating to my trailer room, I sat slumped over on the bed with my thoughts, tuning out the constant whapping of helicopter rotors overhead. Staring into space, wondering what I was even doing here, I absorbed the sound of explosions within and beyond the perimeter that separated Camp Liberty from the sprawl of Baghdad. They'd become white noise by now, static fuzz that kept the trailer from feeling too quiet.

My roommate had been sent home a few weeks earlier following an affair with a higher-ranking officer which necessitated her immediate return to the States to give birth. The unit hadn't filled her bed yet, leaving me with my very own eight-by-ten, combat-adjacent, private room. At times it felt like a tiny palace, but for all the space she'd taken up, my old roommate was also a friend, quick to empathize when I returned from my shift exhausted and overwhelmed, and even quicker to lend a therapeutic foaming face mask. Her absence in my despair made the half-empty room my own personal tomb.

My eyes wandered from the imitation-wood-paneled walls to the floor, across the locally-made rug I'd picked up at the bazaar—a rug that had become coated, like everything else, with the customary combination of dust, sweat and hair. My gaze landed on my roommate's wall locker, whose doors refused to close. Packing in a hurry, she'd left random belongings bursting out of it for me to sort through.

Among the half-empty shampoo and lotion bottles, uneaten care-package candy, stacks of baby wipes, pile of protein bars, and box of ten-for-a-dollar black market DVDs, she had unceremoniously dumped seven magazines, the kind that would normally hold her allotted two hundred and ten rounds of ammunition—if those rounds hadn't been spilling out of a plastic bag sitting casually at the bottom of the locker. I hadn't had a chance to turn them in for her yet, and nobody had come looking for them. In the corner next to the locker leaned my M16. I let my eyes rest on it.

Two hundred and ten rounds, added to my own unused magazines, meant this room contained four hundred and twenty potential deaths. Or just one. I eyed my assault rifle and let my mind wander.

I'd signed up for five years of excitement and exploration, not mental stagnancy and domestic drama. I'd tried so hard to engineer my life intelligently—and where did it get me? Sitting alone in the dark on a dusty bed in Baghdad after working all day for a mission I didn't believe in, sending money home to a man who didn't believe in our relationship, a solution had floated into my head: Why not pick up that rifle and put myself out of my misery?

I let the notion roll around my brain for a minute, absentmindedly measuring the distance from the trigger to the barrel, the distance from my fingers to my head. How would that even work? I'd have to use my toes, stick the barrel in my mouth ... were my legs even long enough?

BEEP BEEP BEEP BEEP BEEP

My alarm clock, ignorant of life-quitting fantasies, yanked me back to a reality where I was still very much alive—and expected at work in twenty minutes.

I slid off the bed onto the floor. My uniform blouse, trousers, boots, and patrol cap lay crumpled in a submissive pile, waiting to be pulled onto my unwilling torso, legs, feet, and head like a shroud. Just like every day, I went through the motions: granny panties, sweat-wicking sports bra, brown t-shirt, black socks, trousers, blouse, tightly-wound bun, patrol cap and boots with the laces tucked in.

Dog tags in left rear trouser pocket, ear protection attached to belt loop, security badge in right breast pocket. Cigarettes and lighter in left cargo pocket, desert-camouflage ID wallet, notebook and pen in right cargo pocket. All pockets checked. I stood up and looked down at my rifle, still leaning disinterestedly on the wall, its muzzle pointing properly toward the ceiling.

Swinging its sling over my head, I let the weapon drop into place on my back, muzzle smacking my calves as it fell into position. Its buttstock rested uncomfortably on my back, jabbing into the edge of my shoulder blade, a bulky reminder that if the terrorists attacked, I would be ready. Against any other enemy, I was on my own.

—

Even from a world away, in the middle of Iraq, I'd known going home to him would present its own set of battles. I could read the nearly-neon signs of a husband who was not interested in being married, but even more brightly shone the warning lights in my mind every time I envisioned the results of initiating a divorce while he was still guardian of all the belongings I'd left behind during deployment. Deciding my best course of action was to try and persuade my wayward man to wait and see how things went once I got home, I shared my decision with the strangers on the internet who, by now, felt like my only friends.

"PUSH HIM INTO TRAFFIC," they responded unanimously.

"I see where you're coming from, but ..."

"TRAFFIC."

"It's just that, you know, he can be really sweet sometimes."

"PUSH HIM."

"And he did say he wouldn't see her anymore ..."

"LET US HELP YOU."

Their words had fallen on blind eyes. It was a week before Christmas. Calling from Camp Liberty, I'd tearfully convinced my husband to give it one more try. My internet friends didn't try to talk me out of it, although their collective sigh of disapproval was nearly audible through the ether. Very softly, so low I could hardly hear it, a small, faint, familiar voice in my head murmured its soft refrain, "You know ... this might be a terrible mistake."

Everything was going to be fine, I decided with a renewed resoluteness. Once we were together, on the same continent, the same side of the world, the same time zone—the same house!—we could have a normal relationship, whatever that was, and we would be nice to each other. How hard could that be? We weren't the first married soldiers who'd been separated by deployment. Every military couple dealt with some kind of marital drama under these circumstances. We would work ours out.

If worse came to worst, I knew who I could call to help me push him into traffic.

———

Our fights weren't about anything as much as they were about everything. Who's better at saving money, who does more house chores, who buys better groceries, who likes the shittier movies, who has terrible taste in music, who shouldn't be drinking an entire handle of whiskey in one night, etc. They never were resolved as much as temporarily left alone once we got too tired or drunk or had to leave for work. We'd inevitably pick up where we left off, and it was only a matter of time before tempers escalated.

In the beginning he only punched my legs and torso, so as not to inflict visible bruises. The first time it happened, I almost called the police. But an arrest would mean our commanders getting involved. After a year of having the military all the way up my ass during deployment, the prospect of having my personal life taken over by my chain of command was somehow more terrifying than being beaten by my spouse. Besides, I was a soldier, wasn't I? I could handle some knocking around.

One Friday night after work, I got a phone call from a friend who used to live in the barracks with us, but had since been moved to a different duty station. She was coming to town for the weekend, she said, did we want to meet up for a drink?

"Let's go out with Nicole!" I entreated my husband. He'd gotten home from work an hour earlier and had already made three inches of whiskey disappear from his newly-cracked fifth of Crown Royal without even enlisting the aid of a glass.

"I don't want to go out with her," he grumbled. "You go without me."

"But I've barely seen you all week. Just come out for one drink. It'll be fun!"

"I can drink here. See? I'm already doing it."

"Oh, come on. She'll be here to pick us up in a few minutes, you won't even have to drive."

He rolled his eyes and took another swig from the bottle. The doorbell rang.

"Dude!" Nicole's voice boomed as I swung open the door. "How the fuck are ya? You ready to go?"

"Dude! Yeah, just give me a minute. The guy's not feeling a night out, but maybe I can convince him."

"All right, hurry up. I'm thirsty."

Down the hall in the bedroom, my drunker half had settled in with the TV.

"Hey, we're about to go. Just come out for one drink. I promise we can go after that."

He picked himself up from the bed, steadying himself as he stood, and lurched toward me. "I told you I don't want to go," he slurred.

"I know you don't, but it's just for—"

CRACK. The room went fuzzy. Pain shot through my face—a face that, until now, had never received an uppercut to the jaw. As my surroundings came back into focus, I saw him slump back onto the bed. His left hand still held the whiskey bottle. "Bitch, I told you NO."

I licked my lips and tasted blood. There was something crunchy on my tongue. Was that …?—I spat into my hand—yes it was. "You broke my fucking *tooth*!" I sputtered. "What the fuck?!"

His eyes were glazed over, mouth twisted into a scowl. "Shut the fuck up and go out with your friend."

"Dude, what's going on?" Nicole called out from the living room. "Are you coming? Megan's gonna meet us at the bar. She's already on her way."

Shaking with rage, I stormed out of the bedroom and back down the hall. When she saw me, Nicole's eyes widened. "What the *fuck*?!"

"Don't worry about it." My jaw throbbed, but now I was too angry to feel pain. "That fucking bastard."

"Okay, we need to go right now. Fuck him, you're coming out with me."

"Dude, I can't go out now. My face is all messed up."

"Are you fucking kidding me? He punched you in the fucking face! You can't stay here!"

I knew she was right, but my head was swimming. How could I go out like this? I shook my head. "No, I can't. You should just go. I'll stay here and ice my face."

"But—"

"Look, I can't go out with a fucked-up face. If someone sees me like this, they'll want to know what happened. The police will get involved."

"Yeah, well ..."

"Yeah, well, fuck no! I don't want to deal with my chain of command over this!"

"Dude. He punched you. In the face."

I collapsed onto the couch. "Go without me. Tell Megan I'm sorry I missed her."

"She's going to be fucking pissed at him."

"I know."

"She's going to want to come back here and beat his ass."

"You know she won't do that. She doesn't want her command getting involved either."

"Dude. You can't stay here."

"Just go, I'll be fine."

She shook her head disapprovingly. "It's really not a good idea for you to stay here."

"It's fine," I repeated. "I'll just sit and watch TV. He's probably passed out by now. I can't deal with this tonight. Just go."

Nicole gave up. "Fine. Fine. Sit here. Just promise you'll call me if anything else happens."

"I promise. Don't worry. I'll be okay. But I can't have anyone finding out about this or I'll have to deal with the company commander all up in my shit."

She shook her head again. "I don't know, dude. I still think you shouldn't stay here."

I sank into the cushions and closed my eyes. "It'll be fine. I'll call you if anything else happens."

She sighed. "All right. Your decision. But you better fucking call me."

"I promise."

The door clicked shut behind her. Exhaustion washed over me. My last conscious thought of the night floated to the surface: *Shit, I need to go buy some makeup before Monday.*

———

My first-line supervisor, Sergeant MacDonald, is a Mormon. I'm not saying that had anything to do with his reaction to my bruises, but none of the other, non-Mormon, soldiers in the public affairs office achieved anything close to a less-appropriate response.

"Whoa, what happened to your face?"

"I … fell into a table." I felt it was the most credible alibi, but, even as well-known as I was for being comically clumsy, most of my colleagues weren't buying it. They'd heard the angry lunch-hour phone calls. It was no secret that my marriage had a solid foundation of conflict. None of them seemed especially surprised that the next step in our journey included visible bruising. Besides, they were well-trained junior-enlisted soldiers—nobody wanted to get involved. The only one who hadn't figured out I'd fallen into a fist was Sergeant MacDonald.

"Wow. That looks really bad."

"I know, Sergeant, it—"

"Can I take a picture of it and use it to make a domestic violence PSA for the newspaper?"

I closed my mouth mid-sentence. Was he fucking with me? That would be a low blow, even for us normally-ruthless public affairs soldiers, the least team-oriented types in the military.

"Um …"

"I mean, you don't have to, but it really looks perfect." He wasn't joking, I realized. Unless I wanted to blow my own alibi, I'd have to play along.

"Uh, sure, Sergeant. Go for it."

"Great! Here, sit in the light."

Snap. Snap.

"Awesome. Got it. Thanks!"

I sighed. "You're welcome, Sergeant." At least I knew he'd stay out of my business.

———

My husband's fuse shortened. It got harder for me to tell when his temper would spark. I don't remember what we were arguing about when his hands around my throat one night caught me off guard, as did the words he spat into my face: "Stupid cunt." My palm flew up before I could stop it. I felt my pinky nail scratch his cheek on its way across his face.

He loosened his grip on my neck and grinned with narrow eyes. "Oh, now you're going to get it." Pushing me down onto the stain-riddled living room carpet of our dimly-lit apartment, he pulled his phone from his pocket. "I'm calling the police."

I scrambled to my feet. "What the fuck! I barely touched you!"

"You cut my cheek. I'm bleeding." A single drop of blood was pushing its way through a tiny scratch. I gaped at him.

"You can't call the police on me for that."

"Watch me." He dialed.

I grabbed at his phone. "What the fuck is wrong with you?"

He cackled and dodged my reach. "Hello, 911? I need to report a domestic violence incident."

"Motherfucker!" He was actually doing it. Could he do this? My heart felt like it was trying to escape my body through my throat. He couldn't do this. I was the one with bruises all over my body. I'd just show them to the police. They'd have to believe me.

—

The holding cell was cold. Fluorescent lights bounced off its once-white walls. I had no idea how long I'd be waiting, only that the military police were on their way and I'd eventually be released into their custody. I shuddered, incredulous to find myself sitting in this stark metal-and-concrete room. The police had believed me. But as they cuffed my wrists and walked me to the squad car, they told me their opinions didn't matter.

"Those are old bruises on your legs," one of them said. "The scratch on his face is new."

"Besides," the other officer chimed in, "you would've had to be the one calling."

I hadn't been the one to call. I'd been the one who waited in the living room, sweating and pacing, cursing him and knowing I couldn't go anywhere, not once he'd talked to the operator. I'd been the one who counted on innocence mattering. This was my first time in a relationship that involved law enforcement—I didn't know the protocol. Alone in the cell, I wondered if my personal survival mechanisms had somehow been disabled. Why hadn't I run? Why was I even still living with this person? Didn't my brain want, at least on some level, to keep my body safe?

The last time I remembered being concerned with my own safety was before Basic Combat Training. When I'd allowed the Army recruiter to lure me into enlistment with promises of college money and all the ill-advised decisions my little heart desired, it had crossed my mind that being sent off to war, even as a public affairs specialist, could result in injury or death. But I was nineteen then. The idea hadn't occurred to me that I'd make it through my first combat deployment only to be taken down by one of my fellow soldiers—especially not one I'd married. Drill sergeants had constantly reminded me that "Pain is weakness leaving the body!" as they prepared me to forego my own health and well-being in the interest of accomplishing the mission. Was I treating my marriage as a mission to be accomplished?

Before I could come to any definitive conclusion, the cell door opened. A military policeman stood on the other side. I heaved a sigh. Life was already painful. Now it was also going to get painfully complicated.

———

It finally dawned on Sergeant MacDonald that my bruises may have been man-made when I showed up at our unit's morning formation exhausted, in someone else's car, with a police report. He sent me to the company commander.

I sheepishly explained the situation to the captain. There was a long pause.

"Do you intend to leave your husband, soldier?"

"Sir, it's all just a big misunderstanding. We'll work it out."

The commander, a large, burly man with a boyish face that somehow didn't yet reflect his many deployments, cocked his head to one side with a grimace. His visible annoyance was tinted with concern. We were no strangers to one another—we'd been deployed together for a year. He knew from experience that I was not skilled at reacting wisely to provocation.

"Soldier, you know I have to advise you against that."

"Sir, I appreciate that, but ..."

"And I'm also going to have to take some preventative action for your safety."

"Sir, I'm sure that won't be necess—"

"Oh, it's necessary. And it's not optional. I'm assigning you a barracks room. You're not going back to your apartment for thirty days. Until then, you're only authorized to see your husband at approved times and locations."

"Sir, the barracks? *Me*??"

"And you're going to a three-day marriage counseling class. Go sign up for it after you leave my office."

"Sir, I promise it won't happen again."

"You're fuckin' right it won't. I'll make sure of that. Go sign up for the class and then get back to work. I don't want to see you in here for this shit again."

"Roger, sir." My face flamed with shame and indignant fury as I made my exit, nearly neglecting the customary salute. This was exactly the consequence I'd feared: a disruption of the small semblance of control I still had over my life. Going to court for a reactionary slap was one thing, but to be moved back to the barracks while he stayed in our apartment—and to be ordered to a mandatory military group therapy session—felt more shameful than a chipped tooth.

I remembered my old roommate MacLane telling me her theory on situations like this while we were in public affairs training. When the drill sergeants had discovered we'd bribed the new privates to stuff our beds before Friday night bed-check so we could stay out at the bar, we'd had our off-post privileges revoked and our civilian clothes taken away. "It's like an idiot tax," she'd said. "You know. The price we have to pay for getting caught doing something stupid."

Outside the company headquarters, I dragged myself over to the smoking area and slumped onto a bench, lighting my tenth or twelfth cigarette of the day. A few of my friends from the company's admin section were already clustered around the ammo-can ashtray. One of them, Clifton, glanced over at me. "You look shitty," he announced mid-exhale.

"Yeah, well, I'm an idiot." Clifton took another drag and gestured around the smoking area.

"So? We all are. We joined the Army, didn't we?" Nobody argued.

"I guess you have a point there."

"Goddamn right I do. Join the fucking club." He smashed the butt of his cigarette into the side of the ammo can and threw it onto the ground. "We're all idiots together."

I mulled Clifton's theory over in my mind as he tromped back into the building, his eyes glazed over with a translucent film of apathy. Viewed through that lens, my future seemed dim. I suspected he was trying to reassure me that we were all in this together. Instead he'd just reminded me that we couldn't help but drag each other down. I could only imagine what the military marriage class would be like. In my mind's eye all I could see was the blind leading the blind. Not even my friends on the internet could save me now.

April 27 –

My marriage-fixin' class is now complete, and I have a fancy certificate to prove it, but my marriage is not fixed. But I did get a lot out of the class! Like, I learned that if my commander thinks he is going to chapter me out of the Army under the Lautenberg Amendment (which, in a nutshell, states that a soldier convicted of a domestic violence charge may not carry a weapon and therefore, cannot be in the Army), he is more wrong than a shit-flavored doughnut, because I was not convicted, so that bitch doesn't apply to me. And, although I intensely want out of the Army, I do not want to get out with a dishonorable discharge. Not after all the insanity I've already come through.

Just one more year till I get out. I can do this.

My character's words are still playing back through my brain weeks later. We're sitting at a picnic table in the barracks courtyard. It's a warm fall day. The sun is shining much too brightly. He squints at me through bloodshot eyes. I turn my head away from him. The sun catches the right side of my face, where the bruises are darkest. I had been in the driver's seat.

"I did that to you?" I nod. A pained look crosses his face. "Fuck. I'm sorry, baby."

"You don't remember?" He frowns and shakes his head. "Not at all?"

"I was so drunk." He *had* been so drunk. "Baby, I promise I'll never do anything like that again. I'll stop drinking. I'll go to AA."

"You really don't remember what happened?"

"I don't remember anything after we left the bar." I believe him. If he didn't remember, he must not have meant it. He hadn't remembered breaking my tooth, either. He'd apologized profusely. A Good Christian Girl™ would forgive him.

"You didn't want to leave the bar. Do you remember not wanting to leave?"

His brow furrows. "Yeah, I think so."

"Do you remember what you did when we were walking to the car?"

"No ..."

"Do you remember grabbing me by my hair and pulling me to the ground on my back?"

He grimaces. "No."

"Do you remember getting into the passenger seat?"

"No."

"Do you remember calling me a stupid bitch while I was driving?"

"No."

"So you probably don't remember me reminding you that you said you wouldn't talk to me like that anymore." He shakes his head. "Right, because that was what happened right before you started punching me in the side of the head."

"Baby ..."

"What *do* you remember?"

He shifts his weight on the bench. "I woke up in a cell. The MPs came and got me. I don't remember anything before that."

I fill in the blanks. I recount how he'd kept punching me while I held my foot on the brake, while I'd screamed for help, which arrived moments later in the form of a woman passing by on the dark street who'd yanked his door open. He'd taken off running. She called 911. The police arrived. They took his description. We received word of his apprehension while they were still collecting our statements.

I'd wanted to drive home, I tell him, but the woman who'd pulled him out of the car had insisted I stay with her for the night. I was too tired to argue. She made me a bed on her couch. I slept till sunrise. She was still asleep when I woke. I left her a thank-you note, stumbled out to my car, and drove myself home to pass out for the rest of the day.

His expression is solemn when he takes my hands. "Baby, I never meant to do anything like this to you." His eyes search deep into mine. My shoulders relax.

"I know you didn't mean to ..."

"I was so drunk."

"I know ..."

"Look at me. This is never going to happen again. I promise." His gaze is set on my face, unwavering. "I love you and I'm going to get help."

My face hurts. But… I raise my eyes to meet his. "Seriously?"

"Seriously. I don't want to hurt you." I allow him to put his arms around me. My shoulders lose a bit more of their stiffness. "I'll stop drinking."

If he stops drinking, we can still get through this. I won't have to rely on random women on the street to save me from the crazy, angry, drunk man in the passenger seat. The thought calms me. We won't have to go through a messy divorce, after all. Life can be better.

Already the memory of waking up with a swollen face on a stranger's couch is fading. I didn't even remember the woman's name … her address … her street.

His arms tighten around me. "I'm so sorry, baby. You know I love you."

"This is insane …"

"We'll be okay! I'll get help. We can go back to counseling."

"Do you mean that?"

"Of course I do. This has been a wake-up call. I need to get help. I love you so much."

"I love you too. I want you to get help." *Everybody makes mistakes.*

"I don't want to hurt you again."

I lift my heavy head from his chest and meet his eyes. Those deep brown eyes. You're full of shit, I want to say, but all that comes out is a sigh.

He kisses my forehead. I close my eyes.

When I open them again, I don't look into his face and tell him, in no uncertain terms, that *damn straight* he won't be able to hurt me again. I don't tell him that I am pressing charges. I don't stand up, sneer at him through my bruised lip, and give him my best, blackened side-eye before striding confidently away from him forever.

I open my eyes and I hear myself whisper, "Okay. Let's give it another try."

I crush the fear that rises in my throat. *When I tell strangers on the internet about it, it'll be funny.* My family, friends, and fellow soldiers might know me as the mess I am, who keeps going back to the same danger like it'll be safe this time. But for my dear, sweet strangers—the friends I don't have to see—I'll spin story after hilarious story, detailing the zany mishaps of the silly character I'm pretending isn't me. I'll leave out the bruises, and together, we'll laugh so I don't have to cry.

I DON'T BELONG HERE

My brain tells me it's the Saturday before a four-day weekend, but the baby-blue booties barely covering my toes wordlessly communicate that this is not going to be a relaxing holiday. It's not even nine a.m. and I've already had to explain to two doctors, a psychologist, and Master Sergeant Bradley that I truly do not belong here.

"I didn't mean it," I insist to each of them consecutively. "It's all a big misunderstanding." I watch the clock above the door tick away the minutes between their visits, becoming less certain that I'm telling the truth with every passing second. Instead of spending my precious long weekend on my couch, I'm spending it under constant surveillance. "I don't belong here," I repeat, less convincingly every time. "I'm not crazy. I want to go home."

Two doctors, a psychologist, a psychiatrist, and Master Sergeant Bradley respectively emit noncommittal *hmmm*s from concern-shaped mouths sitting benignly at the bottom of the skeptical expressions that never leave their faces.

"Please. Just let me go home."

"You know we can't allow that," each voice reminds me in its own distinctive, irritatingly gentle tone.

"But I didn't mean it. I promise. I told you already—I was just saying it because we were fighting."

"Specialist, we take suicide threats seriously here," the voices reply. "When you say it, we have to believe it."

"Then why can't you believe me now?"

"That's not how it works." The psychologist's baritone has a veneer that straddles the fine line between patient and patronizing. "Try to relax. I'm here if you need to talk."

"I can't relax. I don't want to talk. I want to go home. He should never have called you."

"You don't believe he was concerned for your safety?"

"No. He was trying to get rid of me."

"Why do you feel he was trying to get rid of you?"

"He called you to get me out of the apartment. So he could go back to it without me there."

"You don't believe he was worried about you?"

"No. He's an asshole."

"You don't think he took you seriously when you told him you wanted to kill yourself?"

"It doesn't matter. He doesn't care whether I do or not. If he cared, he would have stayed on the phone with me instead of hanging up on me and calling you."

"Are you saying you're still considering it?"

"I wasn't considering it! I told you!"

"Specialist, I'm here to help you."

"I don't want your help. I want to go home."

"You know I can't release you for at least seventy-two hours. If you decide you want to talk, just call one of the nurses and they'll come get me."

"I don't want to talk. I want to go home. This is bullshit."

"There's no need to curse, Specialist. You're here because we want to help you."

"I'm here because my asshole husband wants to fuck with me."

"Nobody here is trying to *eff* with you, Specialist."

"I didn't say you were. *He* is. I told you. I don't want to die."

"Well, that's very good to hear."

"So, let me go home."

"Specialist, you're not going anywhere until Tuesday at the earliest. Demanding to go home isn't going to get you there. I suggest you try to relax. Spend your time here taking advantage of the help we're offering you. When you want to talk, we'll be here to listen."

"Fuck this. I'm not suicidal. I don't belong here."

"Try to get some rest. You had a long night."

"I can't rest here. I'm in a fucking Army mental hospital. Who can rest in an Army mental hospital?"

"When you want to talk, we'll be here to listen," he repeats, emphasizing every word as if in response to a silently cued, *One more time, with feeling!*

I can't help but let out a snort. I've been in the military long enough now to know that the last person I should ever speak with about my mental health is an Army shrink. I might as well talk to myself—that way there'll be no mandatory pharmaceuticals waiting for me at the end of the conversation, and at least I know I'll listen. Besides, how can I expect anyone else to understand how I ended up in this nightmare, if I can't get the message through to myself?

This is what you get for not leaving him, my inner voice softly pipes up before I can silence it. *This is what you get for believing him when he said he loved you.* I try to shut it down, but now it's on a roll. The floodgates are open and there's nothing left for me to do but drown in its torrent. *This is what you get for wanting something better than a miserable existence in those shitty barracks, surrounded by drunks and abusers. This is what you get when you marry another soldier for a better life. This is what you get for not fully committing to cheating the system. This is what you get for your ridiculous honesty. This is what you've earned.*

———

Psych ward nights bring an even more ominous darkness than the ghostly dim that settles every evening over Savannah's creepy trees, branches dripping with Spanish moss as they stand watch over the haunted streets of this storied city I've called my home-away-from-war for nearly four years. Even in fully-lit rooms full of blinking and beeping machines, it's a thicker, heavier night than any I've ever felt in my cozily-furnished apartment or in the barracks, with their ever-illuminated Beige Mile of concrete hallway, and it falls like a brick on my terrified head. Nobody sleeps soundly in a psych ward. Sorrow seeps through the walls, turning every dream into a nightmare. Fear creeps in through every barred window. Depression slides in under every heavy door. I can no longer tell which howls and screams and cries are in my head.

The daytime is nothing but hustle and bustle and bright lights and white coats, but night provides cover for the demons I've spent my whole life wrestling, the kind who never need rest and are always ready to battle to the death. I have no phone with which to seek connection, no TV to drown out the voices in my buzzing brain, no books to fill my mind with fictional problems and displace the drama that my own life seems to have suddenly become.

Or has it always been this way? I escaped reform school at eighteen, only to sign my military contract at nineteen, my marriage license at twenty-one, and my first last-will-and-testament at twenty-two. How did that happen? As my life's high-and-lowlights race across my tirelessly pacing mind in the darkest hours of the night, I comb my memories for answers.

—

I see myself at freshly-seventeen, sitting in the backseat of an SUV, with a man driving, and a woman in the front seat. Their names are long-forgotten—we'd only just met. My parents had introduced us in our living room, where our pastor and his wife also sat.

"These folks are going to take you to visit a school," my dad had said.

"A high school? Why? I just took my GED test."

"Well, just go check it out. See if you like it."

There couldn't be any harm in appeasing him, I'd figured, and agreed to go, with the caveat that I'd be home in time for my five p.m. shift at the Original Cookie. I'd finally settled into a job I liked, with a genial manager and co-workers who had become fast friends. I didn't want to risk losing it all by being late.

"Oh, you'll be back in plenty of time. It's not that far."

An hour and a half later, I'd been chatting so animatedly with the couple in the front of the SUV that I hadn't noticed how far we'd traveled. Before I could ask how much longer we'd be on the road, they handed me a sack lunch. It was a peanut butter and jelly sandwich, and some chocolate peanut butter cups—my favorite—that I decided to save for the ride back. Another half-hour passed. We exited the highway and turned onto a rural road, then another one. As we made our final approach, down a long stretch of gravel, the woman in the passenger seat pointed out the window. "This place is really beautiful—see the soccer field, on the hill there?"

I didn't disagree with her. It was a sunny, crisp, early-October day, and the cloud-dotted, bright-blue skies against the green, rolling hills of upstate New York set a scene so idyllic I could almost hear a trilling flute, welcoming us to The Countryside. But when I got out of the SUV beside a sign for The Family Foundation School, something seemed ... off. *What is this place? And what is going on with those stairs?*

We'd parked at the base of a long, steep set of steps that climbed, ziggurat-style, up the side of a hill. When we reached the top, I was winded. Struggling to catch my breath, I followed my escorts through two sets of doors. My eye caught the sign in the school's entrance: a triangle inside a circle, with the words Honesty, Purity, Unselfishness, and Love wrapping around the circumference. *This is even creepier than church. I am definitely not going to school here. How soon can I tell these people it's time to go?*

The man and woman told me to wait in the main office while they checked us in for our visit. A few minutes later, I was led to a smaller office. A kind-faced, gray-haired woman walked in. I could swear her eyes sparkled as she greeted me. *Aw. It's Mary Poppins' auntie.* I was reflexively returning her smile when she spoke:

"Hi! I'm Susan. I'm going to be your mom!"

Reality screeched to a halt. My throat closed for what felt like minutes before I found my voice. "Um. What?"

"For the next eighteen months, honey. That's how long you'll be here."

"Um. No. I have to go back to Syracuse. I have to work at five." Susan chuckled. "Oh, dear. No, you won't be going to work. Our program is at least a year to eighteen months long." As she spoke, I saw two teenage boys walk in carrying a trunk, with a turquoise-and-purple duffel bag that looked like mine. Was that ...?

"I didn't agree to this!"

"Oh, I know, dear." Susan smiled again. Who was this sweet-voiced woman, and why was she being so cruel?

"Don't I get a phone call? Let me call my parents!" Out of the corner of my eye, I saw a large, bearded man emptying my purse onto a table. "Hey! What are you doing? That's my purse!"

The man guffawed. "Ha! Oh, you new students are so funny. You're not getting this back!" I whipped my head back to Susan, and she was still smiling.

"Oh, no, dear." She let out a lilting laugh. "This isn't jail. You don't get a phone call. Your parents know exactly where you are. You can talk to them at your first family seminar, in thirty days. For now, Tasha and Christine are going to get you settled in."

Two tall, older-looking girls bounded into the room, accompanied by another smiling, middle-aged woman, who introduced herself as Nanci. "Hi, Susan! Is this the new intake?" one of the teens asked.

"Yes it is, girls! You know what to do—get her oriented."

"We're on it!"

Tasha and Christine led me out of the office with Nanci close behind, and brought me across the hall to a women's locker room. "Take off all your clothes," Tasha instructed. I gaped at her. She laughed. "Just do it! Come on, settle down, let's get this done. We have to search you, then we can take you up to the dorms and get you de-loused."

De-loused? What kind of—I realized I was shaking, my eyes wide and heart racing.

After the strip-search, they told me to get in the shower and wash my hair. Once I was clean, Christine sat me down in front of her and dragged a fine-toothed comb coated with Nix Ultra-Lice Shampoo down my scalp while she and Tasha filled me in on the rules. From now on, I would never be allowed to be alone, not even in the bathroom. I would do as I was told by staff and senior students. I would do nothing, not even relieve myself, without permission.

The school was run by a staff of recovering alcoholics and addicts, they said, and its program was based on Alcoholics Anonymous.

"But I'm not addicted to anything."

"That doesn't matter!" They giggled.

I would be expected to memorize and live by the Twelve Steps of AA. I would prepare to have my every thought and action scrutinized, and to do the same to my fellow students. I would maintain a C average in classes, as that was considered passing here. Failure to meet the requirements and follow the rules precisely—not only in academics, but in daily life—would be met with creative "sanctions," such as forced silence, manual labor, or sitting in a corner, facing the wall, with no shoes on. Noncompliance was not an option—students were expected to not only follow, but enforce the rules with one another. If I did noticeably well, I would be rewarded with special privileges and status. If I didn't, I would be swiftly corrected. The girls emphasized that I would have no personal space here, no personal time, and no credibility.

"You know how when you're arrested, you're innocent until proven guilty?" Tasha chirped. "Here, it's the opposite—you're guilty until proven innocent. And you stay till you finish the program, even if you're over eighteen." She and Christine were eighteen and nineteen, respectively. Tasha had been here for three years; Christine, nearly four. My brain, in a last-ditch effort to save my psyche, stopped listening.

I could faintly hear the sound of Tasha and Christine's incessant giggles, blanketed by Nanci's reassurances that I would get used to it, and then, even fainter, my own voice, repeating *Oh my god Oh my god Oh my god* as it sank in like an anvil that my escorts were gone, my parents had lied—and this was my life now.

———

After nineteen months of nearly every test my mental and physical endurance could take, I'd been on the verge of graduation when the staff and my fellow students decided that although I appeared to be doing well, there was just one little thing: I was too sarcastic. I needed to be cured of this character defect before I could be considered ready to rejoin the world outside the school.

They discussed my fate during dinner. I stood before them at the open end of a U-shaped table, hands submissively clasped in front of me, chin dipped at an appropriately respectful angle, as we were all expected to do when it was our turn to stand in front of the Family. Students and staff took turns speaking to and about me, speculating with straight faces about which of the seven deadly sins were responsible for my sarcasm. I offered as many options as I could conjure, hoping that my willingness to be fixed would inspire the Family to show me mercy.

"You're just trying to tell us what we want to hear, so we'll let you off the hook," came the collective rebuttal. "You just want to get over on us, so you can graduate and leave." They weren't wrong. I didn't see sarcasm as a problem—at worst, it was a coping mechanism. Still, I would have gladly shelved it, if I could have, until I'd received the decorative high-school diploma I'd considered hanging alongside my GED on the wall of my college dorm. But the Family wasn't satisfied. If my sarcasm problem wasn't cured here, I would simply "relapse" once I left.

No shit, I must have said with my eyes, clamped-shut mouth fighting every urge to utter a sound, as the Family voted in favor of the Shun sanction. To help accelerate my descent to the "rock-bottom" that would inspire me to change, they decreed I would eat alone, sitting on the floor of the mud room, living and working in silence, forbidden to communicate with or be acknowledged by anyone, staff or student. I would spend my days on a "work" sanction that included picking rocks out of one part of the big, beautiful soccer field, putting them into a bucket, and making a pile in another part of the field, silently. My parents, they said, had already agreed to whatever needed to be done.

This was madness, I knew, but what choice did I have? Yes, by now I was eighteen and free to leave—but where could I go? I had no money, no identification, no transportation, and no destination. My parents had already told me I'd be turned away if I tried to leave the school early and come home. If I graduated, they promised to reward me by sending me to a Christian college, Eastern University, where I'd already been accepted into the journalism program and was expected for fall semester. So, head down, mouth shut, attitude compliant, I took my bucket and headed out to the field.

The only class I was permitted to attend was a gift from a staff member named Neil, a man whose face was fixed in a permanent grimace, lest it betray the kind soul lurking beneath. Neil Dolan was a rail-thin, recovering addict of an indeterminable age somewhere between fifty and eighty. His UV-tinted glasses perched atop a deeply-creased face framed by a spray of gray, frizzy hair that looked like it may have once, many years ago, been blond. His expression said he pitied my predicament, but despite his status as one of my Family Leaders, he'd been unable to sway the others' decision to Shun me. Instead, he'd exercised a rare burst of authority, and insisted that I show up to his folk music class.

Students weren't allowed to listen to music on our own—too many bands were considered "negative," which meant they all were prohibited—so I was elated when once a week, the time came to put down my bucket, broom, or rag and make my way over to the red barn at the bottom of the hill to spend an hour with Neil, a handful of other kids, and a stack of printed music by artists of our parents' generation. Equipped with copies of "Midnight Special" by Creedence Clearwater Revival, "Corrina, Corrina," by Bob Dylan, and "Me & Bobby McGee"—originally written by Kris Kristofferson, Neil huffily informed us, when a student timidly pointed out that another staff member had told us Janis Joplin's music was "negative." We listened to recordings and sang along, one student strumming a guitar. I'd been too relieved to have a break from mindless punitive labor to grasp the full irony of filling that break with choruses of *freedom's just another word for nothing left to lose.*

After three weeks, the sarcasm not shunned out of me, I was informed I'd missed too much school, and now would not be allowed to graduate for another six months. Not only would I miss my first semester of college, but I'd be stuck with the Family until past my nineteenth birthday—a full-grown adult, still subjected to punitive shunning and shaming.

I don't belong here. It was the only thought in my brain on the day I decided it was time to go. Crouched on my knees in the soccer field, sorting through stones while my classmates studied calculus, I concluded that the consequences could be damned. I had to leave to keep a firm grip on my sanity—as far as I could tell, it was all I had left to lose.

On a sunny morning in May, I broke free. I woke up with the rest of the girls in the dorm. I got ready for the day in my usual silence. As the rest of them scrambled to gather themselves for the morning chapel service, an unfamiliar peace settled over me. My face relaxed into a broad smile that none of them could see.

As I walked out the door with nothing but the clothes on my back, a few of the girls figured out what was happening. They broke the Shun sanction to call me back, but I couldn't hear them over the one lyric in my head on repeat: *freedom's just another word for nothing left to lose*. Summoning every tenacious atom in my body, knowing I had nowhere else to go, I hitchhiked to my parents' house, where they informed me, as expected, that journalism school was now off the table. Six months later, faced with a future that no longer included an education, the recruiter had called with an offer I couldn't afford to refuse.

The darkness that fills the chemical-scented, never-silent room now holding me captive turns my baby-blue booties to grey, then black, and turns my mind to the ever-pressing questions ringing in my headlike a stuck doorbell: how in the entire fuck did I get here? How do I get out? Catapulted into adulthood wide-eyed and open-armed by those I trusted to lovingly usher me into it, without so much as a pat on the ass for luck, I'd gone and gotten myself sent off to war by my leaders and driven crazy by the person who'd vowed to always protect me. But in the longest hours of the lonely night, on my back in my bed in the psych ward, I know the words I'm once again telling myself are true: *I don't belong here.*

The night sits heavy on my chest, crushing every hope in my heart, leaving no doubt in my overworked mind that I'm destined to spend my days in cotton scrubs and stocking feet. My fate must be to wander these halls, shuffling from one sterile cell to another, until all my pieces finally unravel and become a crumpled heap on the floor, to be swept unceremoniously away by whichever janitor happens to be on duty.

—

Sunday morning comes down like a lead-weighted Johnny Cash chorus, but with no booze to blame for the aching in my head, and no soothing notes to ease the knowing there's no way to hold my soul that doesn't hurt. Most of the staff are off for the long weekend. My fellow inmates play spades while I stare into space, taking stock of each mad moment that led me to this hell. I have no visitors. Tuesday might as well be a decade away. The second-hand makes its rounds on the clock above the door, and with each passing click it sinks in that I no longer believe myself when I tell the doctors that I truly do not belong here.

What if you just tell them you're crazy? The nagging whisper in the back of my mind sends shivers down my spine. *I can't be crazy*, I hear another voice retort. If they think I'm crazy, I'm in for a lot worse than seventy-two hours of this shit. Administrative discipline. Dishonorable discharge. No college money. A black mark on my résumé where "Army public affairs specialist" would otherwise be. *I have to be fine. I have to be strong. I have to be tough. I am not crazy. I am a combat veteran. I am an American soldier.*

I force myself to sleep so I won't be tempted to talk. With each bout of unconsciousness comes dream after tortured dream. The hands on the clock above the door tell me every time I jerk awake, covered in cold sweat, that only an hour has passed since the last time. I clench my fists and smash my eyelids together, willing my clinical surroundings away, welcoming the horrors of my subconscious. None of these nightmares are more terrifying than my waking life.

—

They let me out after seventy-two hours, as promised. I return to work Tuesday afternoon—newspaper layout day. We are, as always, short-staffed. My fellow soldiers ask no questions. By now, they already have all the answers they need, and we have too much work to do to waste any time on conversations about whose spouse may or not beat them, and who may or may not want to get out of the Army with a self-inflicted discharge. We have a mission. We have a newspaper to put together—the morale of the troops must be boosted, say the generals. We have hearts and minds to win. No matter how broken we are, we must not allow our cracks to show. We are soldiers. The information war must go on. The war inside my head will have to wait.

—

He's sitting on the couch in the dark when I open our door with the hand that isn't holding the keys to my new apartment. "You're back late."

"The newspaper took forever, and I had to go check out a place in Hinesville after work. I thought I told you. Did we have plans?" I flip the light switch. The apartment is spotless. A vase filled with yellow roses sits perfectly centered on the coffee table. He never buys flowers. No matter how many times I've asked. My confusion shows. He sighs.

"I guess you forgot what today is."

I rack my exhausted brain and come up empty. He sighs again.

"Our wedding anniversary?"

My weary heart breaks. I drop my aching body onto the sagging cushion beside him. "Baby, I'm so sorry. I've been so busy, I just—"

"Don't worry about it."

"I just … I thought … I'm moving … we're not …"

His eyes blink. His face blanks. "Okay. I guess that's how it is then."

"But … I didn't think … I mean …"

"I said don't worry about it. I'm going to bed."

"I … love you."

His eyes are sheets of black ice. "Whatever."

He disappears into the bedroom, and I bury my face in the roses in front of me. How many times had I pleaded and cajoled for some—*any*—romantic gesture? How many times, in the two eternal years since our wedding, had I cried for any sign of affection? How many letters had I written from Baghdad, describing the despair deepening with each minute of that deployment, desperately waiting for anything resembling love in return? How could I have expected anything but aggression from another soldier as determined as I am to be Fine? How could I have been such a fool? Is it love? Innocence? Genetic stupidity? After nineteen months of tolerating the Family's abuse, I had nearly forgotten how to stand up for myself. Now, after four years of sergeants screaming at me to suck it up and drive on, have I forgotten that it's impossible to drive on in a vehicle that's undeniably broken down?

The answers to all of the questions swirl together and burst forth from my head as hot tears that finally escape my clenched eyelids, away from the watchful lens of the hospital, hidden from the man who now sleeps soundly on the other side of the wall of the apartment that has never truly been my home. When I lift my head, the first flowers he's ever bought me are drenched in the unmistakable evidence that I may be free, but I am millions of miles from Fine.

I don't know how many minutes pass before I pick myself up, turn out the lights, and join him in our bed. There is no clock above our door.

THE WAY THINGS ARE DONE

The first day of my reluctant return from a relaxing Veterans Day weekend is filled with my favorite activity: no work. I want to be relieved, but I know better than to let my guard down—there's no good thing the Army can't ruin.

A couple of representatives from the public affairs branch headquarters have come down to spend the morning briefing us about why our office will never ever be fully staffed, and to try to convince us to re-enlist.

"Look, uh, there's just a lot of, um, restructuring, happening right now," they offer in what I think they believe is an authoritative tone. "Not every section is, um, *supposed* to be full. It's to make the brigade combat teams more, um, *flexible*."

"As opposed to *functional*?" I barely manage to not say, opting for a less-confrontational, "Uh-huh. That's great. Here's the thing—if you want to keep me in the Army, you'll have to assign me to Paradise, with God as my officer-in-charge." They exchange glances that tell me they can't decide whether my offer is schizophrenic, suicidal, or both, and, more importantly, whether this could disqualify me from reenlistment.

I can't be certain this job has driven me entirely out of my mind, but I've been getting the impression for almost four years now that madness will be my final destination. A week ago, we were informed that instead of focusing our newspaper on Veterans Day, we are to concentrate the bulk of it on "Marne Week"—the 3rd Infantry Division's three-day mandatory self-congratulatory festival, to be held the three days before Thanksgiving. When the announcement came, nervous chuckles bubbled up around the room, but died down in a matter of seconds, to be replaced by the pin-drop silence that follows every time we realize that what we just heard was not, astonishingly, a joke. We, a military newspaper, were truly being instructed to put one of the two most significant military days of observance on the back burner and tout a celebrity-stacked carnival in its place.

We all assume our new commanding general is doing this strictly to test our obedience. Why else would the articles we have been instructed to "put off till next week" include local Veterans Day observances and stories about veterans from our own division? Why else would we be replacing them with bios and backgrounds of the performing acts at Marne Week (such as: Leann Rimes! the Miami Dolphins cheerleaders!), a two-page spread detailing the activities of Marne Week, giant flyers advertising Marne Week, and of course, traffic predictions and road closures during Marne Week? Thanks to Marne Week, many people's Thanksgiving weekend passes will be forcibly postponed until Thanksgiving Day, so we can operate at full capacity to carry out Marne Week duties. Every soldier's morale now drunkenly teeters at the edge of a bottomless pit of despair, no longer looking for a lifeline to hang onto … no longer believing there ever was one to begin with.

——

The new lieutenant colonel is considered, by consensus, to be our former lieutenant colonel's D-list replacement. Our old boss only took the job as seriously as he needed to and never minded ruffling a few brass feathers, but Lieutenant Colonel Barton has made it clear that our sole purpose, as his public affairs team, is to appease anyone who outranks him. His birdlike build, while decidedly non-threatening, is paired with a face that seems to be perpetually on the verge of asking you to explain the joke everyone else is laughing at, unaware that the joke is him. He is the unfortunate owner of the type of middle-management personality that stubbornly refuses to be endearing to anyone. We underlings refer to him by many creative nicknames behind his back and defer to him only because mutiny is punishable by, at worst, death. Ever since he refused to run my weekly tongue-in-cheek commentaries in the newspaper, I have not allowed him to make eye contact with me. Despite his much-higher rank, he obliges by keeping his distance, so I alternate between pretending he doesn't exist and shooting invisible, ineffective death lasers at him with my eyes whenever he dares to step into my radius.

"He *really* does not want to deploy with you if he can possibly help it," Sergeant Allen, my new editor, tells me in a low voice after the colonel skulks out of the newspaper office.

"If only he could make such wise choices all the time."

Sergeant Allen snorts. "And break his record of unparalleled idiocy?"

"Which is exactly why *I* really don't want to deploy with *him*, if I can possibly help it."

"Yeah, well, hate to break it to you, but stop-loss is about to stop you from helping it. Better start getting used to it. I am, and believe me, I *really* don't want to deploy with *any* of these assholes."

There's a certain camaraderie that grows like a weed in trauma-bonded combat units, but is nothing short of a rare flower in any given one of the Army's optimistically-named public affairs teams. Unlike infantry teams, which are trained to accomplish missions as a group while keeping each other alive, public affairs soldiers are individually trained to be wherever the military most needs a set of eyes and ears (usually, directly in the middle of an infantry team which has just been instructed to be on its best behavior). We manage to work together when we have to, but, like a roomful of tired toddlers, only a precious few of us ever genuinely get along with each other. I've come to accept that by the time a typical day is over, I will want to cut someone open and feed them their own intestines. I see this as a step forward in my quest for self-realization and inner peace.

"You know that means you, too, right?" Sergeant Allen's voice shatters my moment of zen.

I let out a reflexive snort. "I mean, how could anyone not want to go back to Iraq with a bright ray of sunshine like this one?"

"You think I'm kidding."

"You know? I really don't."

———

Days later, news comes down from headquarters: the general has volunteered our division for what we're being told is a "troop surge."

"It's supposed to help us win the war," Sergeant Allen flips over his shoulder derisively. "Like Iraq needs more soldiers shoved up its ass."

"Do you think it'll work?"

"Work? I don't fucking know. It'll keep us there, that's for sure."

"It'll keep *you* there. I'm getting out."

"Oh yeah? I wouldn't be too sure about that."

"What are you talking about?"

"Uh, stop-loss? You know, that little policy keeping half the division from getting out on time?"

"Don't give me that tone, I know what stop-loss is. I'm getting out before it goes into effect. I've been saving leave days for, like, seven months. I'll be out by April. The division doesn't deploy till July."

"You seem convinced."

"Why are you smirking? Have you heard something else?"

"I mean, I *might* have seen the deployment orders on the colonel's desk."

"What?!"

"And they *might* have said we're deploying in March."

"WHAT."

"So you *might* want to give the branch manager a call and see if he still wants to let you re-enlist, because otherwise …"

"Don't you fucking say it—"

"You're going back to Baghdad with the rest of us unfortunate surging motherfuckers," he cackles.

I drop dazedly into my chair. "No way."

"Oh, yes."

"Fuck."

"Hey, it's getting me, too. I was supposed to get out in May. Now we've got, let's see, according to the orders, an extra year to eighteen months, starting in March."

"FUCK."

"Look, you might actually be able to get out of this thing— didn't Master Sergeant Bradley say they're still looking to fill a slot in DC?"

"Ugh, yes. But I'd have to re-enlist for three years."

"Buuuut you'd never have to deploy with the 3rd ID again …"

"Three years!"

"Is it really that much worse than another *year and a half* with this bunch of douchebags?"

He's not wrong: time does seem to move at half-speed when you're surrounded by people who like you even less than you like them. I emit a defeated sigh.

"Dude, you'll be fine. Go to the retention office at lunch. They'll help you out. They want to keep everyone they possibly can."

"I really hope you're right."

"Hey, if I'm wrong, what's the worst that can happen? They send you back to Iraq?"

"Is that supposed to make me feel better?"

"Good point. Just go to the retention office."

———

It normally takes me till at least Tuesday to recover from my weekend—not in the "sleep it off" sense, as much as the "stop being angry that I can't just call in sick for the two-hundredth Monday in a row" sense. Every day in the Army, another drop of my will to live is noticeably drained. At this point, I'm only barely managing to retain the portion that allows me to see the humor in life's annoyances—it's been nearly overtaken by the portion that causes me to ask our office's graphic designer to create giant posters depicting me dancing merrily around while waving the lieutenant colonel's head around on a stick, as inspired by the most gruesome scene in the director's cut of *Natural Born Killers* that's recently been making its way around Headquarters Company.

We might suspect the new commanding general is testing our obedience, but we are certain the lieutenant colonel is testing our sanity. Every time he makes a decision, our lives are thrown into chaotic disarray.

Sergeant Allen makes up half of our military newspaper staff. The other half is me. There are a couple of civilians who help out regularly, but as far as public affairs soldiers go, we are it. With our powers combined, we've made it clear that we disapprove of our fearful leader's persistent attempts to simultaneously kiss the general's ass and make our lives harder, but the lieutenant colonel's lips have stayed imperviously puckered. After finally picking up on the fact that Sergeant Allen didn't want to work for him, the colonel decided a new job was in order—but instead of reassigning him to one of the unfilled positions already in existence in our division, the colonel chose to create a brand new one.

Now, my former editor is the commanding general's personal official photographer. Every time the general decides he needs one of his actions documented (inspecting buildings, talking to local important persons, picking his nose, etc.), his official photographer will have to be on hand to do it. Our team of two is down to one.

The colonel has been avoiding me since I got off the phone with the branch manager. He knows I'm trying to get out of here. By now, he's heard I've secured the DC position, far away from this division. I just have to sign a reenlistment contract. Soon, the sergeant at the company retention office promised me—he'll have the paperwork ready really soon.

"You know you have to disenroll from the Army Married Couples Program first though, right? Since your spouse doesn't have enough time left in to switch duty stations with you?"

"Oh. Well, I guess ... "

"It's the only way. Otherwise you'll get held up till he gets out. When's that, again?"

"July."

"Yeah, if you wanna get out of here before stop-loss hits, you gotta disenroll. Let me know when it's done."

———

Our marriage is still hobbling along on two broken legs, despite my better judgment, and disenrolling from the program that keeps us stationed together will permanently disrupt our couples counseling, but in the end, the option of not going to war wins the battle in my mind.

A week later, my husband comes home to inform me that he's being moved to North Carolina.

"But don't you have less than a year left in your contract?"

"Yup."

"So how—"

"I don't know, baby. That's just what they told me."

I still don't have my reenlistment paperwork submitted. The stop-loss date is looming. He has to be moved by the middle of January, and we both know once he arrives at his new duty station, he could also get stop-lossed and deployed to Afghanistan, or somewhere equally undesirable. It crosses my mind that a deployment could do him some good, but by now, he's just as sick of the military as I am. We used to have some semblance of control over our own futures, and now, little by little, that illusion is being taken from us.

Master Sergeant Bradley pulls me into his office when I get to work the next day.

"So, Specialist—do you know about the do-not-retain list?"

"Uh, no, Sergeant." I've heard of people being barred from reenlistment, but usually only soldiers who fail PT tests or gain too much weight.

"Well, it seems you're on it."

"Excuse me, Sergeant?"

"I've, uh, been told that you're on the battalion's do-not-retain list."

"I don't understand, Sergeant. I was told everything was in ord—"

"Yeah ... well, it's something about too many counseling statements. Apparently the battalion commander won't sign off."

"But—I haven't gotten a counseling statement in months. Not even the routine ones." Our section has been too understaffed to complete monthly counseling statements. Either way, the person counseling me would have been Sergeant Allen, whose opinion about all behavioral paperwork is that it doesn't matter. My mind darts back and forth between shock and disbelief. *None of this is making any sense.*

"Well, look. Here's the thing. They're willing to give you a trial period."

"A trial period? For what, Sergeant? I haven't done anything—"

"If you haven't done anything it should be easy, right? Just go six weeks without a negative counseling and—"

"*Six weeks?* But the stop-loss order is going to go into effect!"

"Look, I said they're giving you a chance. Do you want it or not?"

"Sergeant, this doesn't make sense. How would I be able to reenlist if the stop-loss order comes down?"

"That's between you and the battalion. Now, do you want the trial period or not?"

If I say no, I'm stuck deploying with these people. If I say yes, I could still get stop-lossed and deploy with them anyway. My heart thuds to the floor under the weight of what I now know is my only real option. "Six weeks?"

"Six weeks."

I tell Sergeant Allen about the latest development in my reenlistment saga when he comes in from a photo shoot with the general's entourage around the post golf course. He raises an eyebrow on a face whose expression is already in a semi-permanent state of cynicism.

"Do-not-retain list? What the fuck is that? I've never heard of that."

"Yeah, me neither. But that's what Sergeant Bradley said."

"I think they're fucking with you."

"Of course they're fucking with me."

"You think they're trying to keep you from leaving?"

"I mean, the colonel doesn't want to deploy with me, right? So I can't imagine why they'd do that."

"Yeah, but he's a dick. What if they just can't find anyone to fill your slot? Do you think they're just saying this shit about a do-not-retain list to cover their asses?"

"I mean … that would be so fucked up."

"Yeah. It would."

We finish our work in silence.

———

The stop-loss order is in effect—it has been in effect, as we find out when we finally see it, for five months. The battalion clerk tells me there's still a glimmer of hope for me to get a waiver to get out of here: all I have to do is get Lieutenant Colonel Barton to grant his permission.

"Really? I was told that if he signs off on my transfer, he won't get a replacement for me in time."

The clerk sucks air through his teeth and clicks his tongue. "Ohhh. That's true. Yeeeeah, no, probably not then, no. Yeah, no, he won't sign. Lieutenant Colonel Barton? Yeah, he definitely won't."

"Uh-huh … thanks."

"Here to help."

It's nearly ten p.m. when I let myself into my apartment. We finished the newspaper late again, following six consecutive hours of briefings about how to evade and/or escape being captured by the enemy (none of which, to my disappointment, refer to the escape or evasion of a soldier's own unit), and my brain is rapidly entering shutdown mode.

As my body hits the couch, my phone rings. There's no name on its LED screen—only the familiar digits of the office phone. I have to answer.

"Hello?"

It's Master Sergeant Bradley. And the lieutenant colonel. The colonel speaks first.

"So, uh, Specialist. What we want to know is, do you want to get out of the Army?"

This is obviously a trick question. "Well sir, I do want to get out of the Army ..."

"So are you saying that you are not willing to be a member of this team?"

What? Where is he going with this? Don't fuck this up, Self. "... but while I'm in the Army I will continue to do my job to the best of my ability." *Was that right?*

The colonel lets out a loud exhale. "Oh good. Because we need an individual of your experience and skill level to deploy with us, but it has been my perception that you are a liability to this team, and I have been planning to tell the battalion commander just that."

Where is this going? "Sir, I can assure you that I am not a liability. I have always and will continue to work just as hard and harder at my job than anyone else in our section, and I think that everyone here can attest to that."

"Well, Specialist, I know you've had issues in the past with certain individuals and certain events in your life, and your NCOIC here has told me that you are continuing to work through them and are progressing. I want to know whether or not I can count on you to be a valuable member of this team."

I am so confused. "Of course you can count on me, sir."

The colonel's voice is suddenly bright. "Okay then! So I will tell the battalion commander that my previous assessment of you was wrong, and that you are prepared to be a part of this mission."

My brain is in full What The Fuck mode. *What is happening right now?* I gulp. "Roger, sir."

"Excellent. So you are going to deploy with us, correct?"

WHAT. IS. HAPPENING. I hear myself answer, "Um ... I guess so, sir?"

"Okay, that's what's happening then. Are you ready to do this?"

NO. NO I AM CERTAINLY NOT. "Yes I am, sir."

He hangs up. I sit quietly for a moment.

Did I somehow ... volunteer for deployment? No ... no. No, I couldn't have. What—really? No. What? Okay. If I said I was a liability, which I'm not, then either I get kept home from deployment—still in the Army—and I catch hell from my supervisors here for being a shitbag. Or, I get deployed anyway and catch hell from my supervisors there for being a shitbag. There was no right answer to that question, was there? OR WAS THERE??

I'm still immersed in variations on this inner monologue a few minutes later when Master Sergeant Bradley calls me back.

"I really appreciate what you just did. That shows me that you are really trying to do the right thing."

That ... I? Am doing the... right thing? But the ... the colonel said ... what? I manage to mumble something reasonably resembling words in response.

"Just keep that attitude and you'll do fine. Goodnight!"

"Good? ... night."

So, here we are. After all this time, jumping through all these hoops, I'm going to deploy again after all. The voice in the back of my head rambles on, reminding me things could be worse—

yes, this deployment is going to be long, stressful, exhausting, and emotionally taxing for me, but I'm not the only one to be stop-lossed. The thought crosses my mind that I would feel like a jackass if I tried to get out of the Army on time while everyone around me shipped out. Even if it was an option, could I bring myself to be *that* soldier?

I'm not deploying because I want to, or because I think it's a good idea. I'm doing it because deep down, I believe that if I don't do it—if I get out of it on a technicality—I will be making light of everyone else's sacrifice. I'll be saying that I am special, that I deserve to stay home when my fellow soldiers pack up and go to war, and that the contract I signed is negotiable.

And no matter how badly I want to, I can't say that. I could have told the colonel that I'd raise hell all tour long, that he'd pray to all the gods to deliver him from my fury, that he'd come home a broken and bitter man ... but I didn't. Without realizing it, despite every effort to resist the Army's conditioning and retain control of at least my own mind, I have suddenly become the kind of soldier the Army has always wanted: even when given the choice, I can't quit the team. It's no longer an option. Maybe it never was. Maybe, without noticing, I surrendered my will along with my body when I took the oath.

Whether I really have to or not, I have to go back to Baghdad.

—

My mother-in-law mails me a book—"reading material for your trip," she says in the accompanying letter—called *Cruel and Unusual: Bush/Cheney's New World Order*, by Mark Crispin Miller. I don't consider myself particularly politically-minded, but I do know I'm getting fucked over, up, and around by my commander-in-chief, so I save the book for the plane—nothing good can come of learning more right now.

——

Our departure date is tentatively set for March 19th, a week away. I haven't gotten anything done on my mental to-do list except "Drown sorrows in alcohol" and "Repeat," and the stress is frizzing my every last nerve. I know that in order to keep myself healthy, I need to calm down and get it all done, but the closer I get to leaving, the more helpless I feel.

It's fully dawning on me that I'm actually going back. I keep telling myself that I'm not going to succumb to depression, or a nervous breakdown, or the urge to just flee! Flee for the border! but every day I become a little less sure about that. There will be rockets and mortars and myriad other explosives, but those fade to the back of my mind as visions of loneliness, despair, and twelve-hour work shifts in brain-melting heat dance a dirge in my head. I can feel my serotonin levels bottoming out.

I tell myself all I need is a decent night of sleep, and I'm almost exhausted enough to believe it.

——

There are fewer than twenty-four hours left before I get on the plane. I am leaning precariously out of my mind's door, danger-ously close to falling out. All of the last-minute deployment prepa-rations are getting slowly but steadily accomplished (including an hourly argument with myself: even though Canada seems like a better alternative, it is, for some reason, not one), and nearly all I have left to do is say a few last goodbyes, stuff a carton of ciga-rettes into my duffel bag, turn in my apartment key, and try not to shed any of those now-habitual unsoldierly tears.

Last time I deployed, I didn't cry. I hugged my husband, threw my bags onto my back, and boarded the bus. The excitement of doing something new and different kept me going for the first, I don't know, three days, before the reality of where I was set in.

Things are different now. I've said all my in-person goodbyes. I'm sure there will be a few phone calls before I get on the plane, but there won't be any pre-departure hugs or waving out of the window. The anticipation that carried me through before is decidedly waned. After all, I'm going back to almost exactly the same place I was before. All I can anticipate now is that creeping sense of involuntary solitude that caught me off-guard in the beginning of the last deployment—because this time, I'm prepared for it. I'll never be surprised again to feel just how alone I really am while I'm supposedly surrounded by my team.

DESPERATE TIMES

Fucking cheerleaders, loops the refrain in my brain, although truth be told, I have nothing against them. I sincerely appreciate not just their unapologetic sexiness, but the way the building feels slightly more cheerful and smells slightly less like man-sweat while they're in it. Even though I can't help but object to using their bodies to boost the troops' morale, I'm not put off by their presence—it's the visit's aftershocks that make its biggest impact: once the cheerleaders leave, there is no way to deactivate the uncontrollable hormone field their arrival inevitably activates. The last time a gaggle of them showed up all spray-tanned, hot-pantsed, and smiling, I introduced myself and my outside voice said, "Hi, I'll be your photographer today." My inside voice added, "Please just take all the male soldiers with you when you go."

The well-known Don't Ask, Don't Tell policy is still in effect, so I'm not worried about unsolicited flirtations from fellow female soldiers. Either way, most women I've met know how to take no for an answer. But we're only four months into the deployment, and the boys are already far too bold for my liking.

"Are you married?" they demand, and if given an affirmative, follow it up with, "Does it matter?"

"YES," I emphatically answer, breaking down my rejection into the smallest words possible. "IT DOES MATTER. GO AWAY." There was a time when I tried to be nice to everyone, but that was before the days of indefinite deployments and cheerleader-inspired corrective training. I have no more energy for nice.

Freedom from the testosterone-soaked stares of male soldiers for an entire morning would be a welcome relief if it didn't mean that once the cheerleaders left, the ogling I normally endure would return ten times fiercer than before. It's like dangling a rare steak in front of a hundred caged sharks, then filling the shark tank with sickly goldfish and hoping all the goldfish will live to a ripe, old age.

Everyone in the headquarters this morning is more obnoxious than ever as they slowly come down from their estrogen high—and once my buddies discover my public affairs office has a color printer, they all want their cheerleader photos printed. At first I maintain a blank expression with my firm stance of refusal, but eventually I can no longer conceal my annoyance. Although my response is always the same ("Sorry, if I do it for you, I have to do it for everyone"), my face inevitably betrays me: "You are an idiot," it says silently and emphatically to each requestor. "A goddamn idiot."

I can't really fault them, I begrudgingly admit to myself. We're all miserable, and the sad truth is that scantily-clad bodies are rare in the dusty, depressing task force headquarters. Men's and women's living quarters are strictly segregated, even for platonic loitering. The commander issued a general order forbidding pornography and fraternizing between genders, and that, combined with the Don't Ask, Don't Tell policy, means the only people who can legally get up to anything non-platonic during deployment are heterosexual troops who are already married … to each other. The rest of us have to seek privacy elsewhere—quarters are tight and walls, when they exist, are thin. I've heard some people are even resorting to the rarely-cleaned portable toilets sprinkled in clusters around the base. These are desperate times … and now some high-ranking officer has decided desperate times call for women in desperately-short shorts. My inner voice groans. I've done this to myself. Sergeant Smankowich's irritated voice is still ringing in my ears. Unlike my alarm clock.

"You're late again, Specialist," he'd snapped as I hustled into the headquarters yesterday morning.

"I know, Sergeant. I slept through my alarm."

"You mean, you slept through your alarm *again*."

"Roger, Sergeant."

"You know I have to give you a written counseling, right?"

"I know, Sergeant, but I don't know what else I can do. I'm a deep sleeper."

"You can get a louder alarm."

"Sergeant, all twenty-five of us in the tent are on different shifts and I can think of at least ten specific people who will hate me for that."

"Specialist, you're already getting counseled for lateness. Don't make me add 'disrespecting a noncommissioned officer' to the list."

"Roger, Sergeant."

"All right, stand at parade-rest."

I sighed.

"Do it!"

"Roger, Sergeant." As instructed, I stood up straight, feet slightly more than shoulder-width apart, interlocked my hands behind my back at the waist, and waited.

"You're being counseled for failure to report to your assigned place of duty in the headquarters public affairs office at the appointed time. This is your third time being late this month and as a result you will undergo the following corrective training: you will complete your regular shift from noon to midnight, then report to the Media Operations Center at zero-nine-hundred with your camera. A group of New Orleans cheerleaders will be waiting to tour Task Force Baghdad headquarters and visit soldiers. Your mission is to photograph their entire visit, print out official group pictures of the cheerleaders with the command team, and contribute a stand-alone photo, with caption, to be used in the daily newsletter, which you will lay out and distribute before the end of your shift as usual. Do you have any questions?"

"Is there possibly anything more degrading I could do instead, Sergeant?"

"Watch it, Specialist."

"Roger, Sergeant."

"I don't care what kind of alarm clock you need to get. You must be on time. Maybe this corrective training will help you remember that."

"Roger, Sergeant."

—

The morning's visit did carry one surprise, I admit to myself as the last grateful soldier walks off with his full-color, glossy trophy. A few men in the headquarters actually didn't fall all over themselves to touch the hem of the cheerleaders' minimal garments. They, like me, had rolled their eyes at the soldiers who threw self-respect to the wind and followed the ladies through the building with faint lines of drool glistening from the corners of their lips.

"Dude. They really made you come in early to take pictures of this shit?" Hamilton from admin had commented, leaning on the wobbly temporary wall that separated his desk from the main hallway, watching his sergeant major clamber to get into the group photo I was attempting to frame.

"Don't get me started," I'd hissed through the grimace I'd been trying to pass off as professional-grade stoicism all morning. "Okay everyone! Smile like you're not deployed!"

"Dude. That's so cold of them."

"Really? I hadn't noticed." Usually I appreciate affirmations of the obvious, but on this day my patience was short. I'd been too worried about oversleeping again to get more than a couple hours of quality unconsciousness in before this shift, and the extra-strong coffee I'd chugged had already worn off. The group giggled its way down the hall, luring soldiers away from their work, a perfectly-manicured flock of pied pipers.

"Your NCOs must really hate you," Hamilton called after me as I hustled to keep up with them.

"You think?" I retorted over my shoulder, his cackle echoing through the building.

At my desk, still cursing the cheerleaders, I upload my photos, adding Task Force Baghdad logos and the command team's names to the images and printing them on glossy card stock as ordered. *Your Tax Dollars At Work,* I'm tempted to add, in barely-legible type, at the bottom.

A dozen toothy, shit-eating grins mock me in two dimensions as I trudge back down the uneven stairs of Saddam's old money-printing factory that our task force took over as its headquarters. I enter the general's office without knocking and drop the photos unceremoniously on the desk of his aide. His aide, the inexplicably friendly Captain Griffin, glances up from his computer screen, first toward me, then down at the pile of glossy paper I've just deposited in front of him.

"Sweet! Cheerleaders! Thanks!"

Grunting a defeated, "You're welcome," I leave the office and shut the door behind me, unable to tell whether I feel better or worse.

———

Months slog by. With the help of a new ninety-decibel, bed-shaking alarm clock aptly named the Sonic Bomb, I manage to consistently get to work on time, but my buddies in the headquarters remain relentless. If they see me in a hurry, they shake imaginary pom-poms and wag their hips. "Hurry up or you'll get stuck on cheerleader duty again!"

I can't stay mad at them. They've now been stuck in the headquarters for more than a year of mindless, mission-driven monotony punctuated by daily incoming mortar-fire. Their brains, like mine, have developed a habit of strategically shutting down in self-defense.

"Cute, guys. Those routines are ready for the Super Bowl."

"You know you love 'em," Hamilton grins.

"Sure. I love 'em at least as much as you love working here."

"That bad?"

"If I'm being honest? Probably worse."

"At least we're all miserable together."

"True. Speaking of which," I lower my voice. They lean in with raised eyebrows. "I happen to have acquired a bottle of something that looks like water but smells suspiciously like vodka."

"Oh really?"

"I could be persuaded to share it if you give your dance moves a rest."

"You make a good argument. Ferguson and me are gonna watch a movie in our room later if you want to bring it over." After more than a half a year we've finally been moved out of tents into trailers, and the relative privacy of two-person rooms in trailers feels like a luxury. Now to avoid getting in trouble for occupying a room with a soldier of another gender, all we have to do is enter and exit the room unseen. Once inside, we can almost convince ourselves we're something like adults, rather than oversized, heavily-armed children with no agency over our own space.

"That could be fun …" *Or not.* We all know what a year without legal sex can do to male soldiers—and it's now been thirteen months.

Stop being paranoid, I chide myself. *These guys are friends. We've known each other for months. We laugh at cheerleaders together.* I let a breath out. The biggest risk here is getting ratted on by some soldier who's jealous we aren't sharing our booze. "Sure, I'm in."

"Come over around 2100. It'll be dark by then, so nobody'll see you."

"All right. What're you watching?"

"We don't know yet. Got anything new?"

Bootleg DVDs are as common here as dirt, and almost as free. My most recent acquisition is still in theaters back in the States.

"I just picked up *Juno* from one of the Hajjis on the camp shuttle." I know we're not supposed to use that word to refer to all Iraqis, but somehow it's slipped into daily use anyway. I make a mental note to use the approved term—"local national"—in the future. It still doesn't sound better.

"*Juno*? Is it good?" Hamilton raises an eyebrow and flashes me a smirk of faux skepticism.

"Sure. It's funny. Watched it with my roommate a couple days ago, but I'd watch it again."

"Okay, bring that. We have some Gatorade from the chow hall we can mix with the vodka."

"Delicious ..."

"What, you got something better?"

"My roommate and I tried it with V8 last night and it was pretty gross so ... no."

"That's what I thought. See you tonight."

———

It's been a bad year for romance. A few months in, my husband and I decided our marriage of two and a half years wasn't going to survive the strain of another deployment, and, in an uncharacteristically even-keeled long-distance call, agreed to put it out of its misery. I've been entertaining myself ever since with anyone who can capture my attention—after all, the pickings are plentiful, if not without blemishes. This is a fifteen-month combat tour and I've had no desire to remain celibate, but I also see no need to drop my standards along with my pants.

I consider the possibility of Hamilton as a prospective friend-with-benefits. He has an appealing face. His eyes aren't entirely glazed over with apathy, though he never seems overly concerned with anything going on around him. But even with those boxes checked, he still faces one insuperable barrier to eligibility: his rank. It's the same as mine. That will never do.

In the interest of discretion, I've narrowed my first choices for casual dalliances down to individuals bound to secrecy due to holding a rank, job title, or marital status that would be critically endangered if we were discovered. I already have one reputation—that of a profoundly disgruntled public affairs specialist—and wear it with pride. But if word gets around that I, a woman, am exercising my sexual freedom with other consenting adults, then I'll be labeled a slut, without the accompanying adoration that title affords my male counterparts.

"Maybe they get respect for it because they have to try harder," my friend Abbott theorizes one night on our walk back from the dining facility, sharing horror stories of same-rank dating and the shaming that resulted. "And they want to hate on us because we don't."

"You think they're just jealous we can be better than they are at slutting with less effort?"

A mortar round explodes in the not-too distance. We scurry to the nearest blast walls just in case the next one comes closer. We change course to walk alongside the barrier.

"Of course they're jealous." Abbott chuckles. "I mean, look around. They're just big little boys with guns."

She and I, along with the rest of our fellow female soldiers, know better than to expect we'll be judged as men's equals, but we also have to dodge the inevitable "bitch" bullets that shoot daily out of the mouths of our male colleagues if we dare express a degree of confidence in our bodies or abilities. Any sign we might also like sex is a guarantee we'll be looked down on by our chain of command, no matter how many diseases the men in our barracks bring home from the strip clubs. But, stigma or not, we're still humans—young humans, at that, most of us in our teens and twenties. Nature requires humans to follow where our hormones lead, and the military requires soldiers to be creative about it.

———

Camp Victory is the home of Multi-National Corps–Iraq, and true to its name, it sucks in soldiers from around the globe. Foreign officers are the preferred population for Abbott's and my "dating" pool, with civilian contractors a close second and U.S. officers (first commissioned, then noncommissioned) trailing behind at a reluctant third. Other enlisted troops might make the cut if they're undeniably charming or uncharacteristically intelligent, but unless being discovered with me will bring them serious consequences, I'm not interested. The perfect partners are attractive, engaging, and at risk of losing everything if they say a word. If they're married, I feel bad for their wives, but my military morality compass tells me what they don't know won't hurt them. Besides, if one of us is killed by an incoming mortar, nobody will be the wiser. Fidelity is negotiable in a combat zone.

The popular justification for affairs among soldiers has been ripped off from a newly-launched Las Vegas marketing campaign: "What happens in Iraq, stays in Iraq." We all agree it has a nice ring to it. Just like everywhere else in the military, the rules are flexible here as long as we don't get caught—and just like everywhere else in the military, there's nothing to be done if, in the course of bending rules, we end up broken.

———

It's already been dark for an hour when I knock quietly on Hamilton and Ferguson's door with a one-liter plastic bottle tucked inconspicuously under my arm. It's warped from the heat—one of those bottles that was baking on a pallet in the sun all day under shrink-wrap, the main source of officially-potable water on base. A few of us suspect the plastic is toxic, especially on triple-degree days when the water in the bottle burns our lips. Their one redeeming quality is their size: perfect for a discreet fifth of liquor.

Nobody is sitting outside when I walk up to Ferguson and Hamilton's door. Since being moved into trailers, we have a fraction of additional privacy, but most hours of the day and night, soldiers in folding chairs with nosy eyes and knowing looks line each row of trailers. Tonight, the neighborhood is empty and quiet. The only sound on the way over was the crunch of my footsteps in the deep-layered gravel that covers every inch of ground around and between every trailer. When the door opens, I slip inside as noiselessly as possible.

"Hey dude," Hamilton greets me with a grin. "Did ya bring the vodka?"

"Uh, yeah. Got the mixer?"

Ferguson produces two sixteen-ounce bottles of Gatorade.

I groan. "Dude. Lemon-lime? That's the nastiest flavor."

"Come on, it's not that nasty. Besides, it was the only kind left in the chow hall at dinner tonight."

"Probably because it's nasty."

"Well you can either have nasty or nothing, so … your call."

I sigh. *I should be used to these choices by now.* "Nasty it is. Do you have cups?"

Red Solo cups are produced from a wall locker and drinks mixed. Seating is more of a challenge. None of the rooms are big enough for more furniture than two people need to sleep and store their belongings, so Hamilton pulls out a collapsible camp chair for himself, Ferguson sits on a foot locker, and Hamilton's twin bed becomes my perch. As the movie opens, we establish the rules.

"The other night, my roommate and I decided the best rule is to drink every time you see yellow shorts." This, we all agree, is the single most-used visual device in the film and thus, the best path to comfortable inebriation. Inebriation, of course, is the primary objective here—the movie is simply a vehicle for this necessary escape from reality's persistent bleakness.

"Works for me. How about you, Ferguson?"

"I'm in."

Yellow shorts abound, and the Gatorade's nastiness ceases to be noticeable. I've already seen this movie, but that becomes irrelevant as each slug of the lemon-lime liquor further heightens its entertainment value. As the plot reaches its peak, I finally feel myself relax.

———

It's dark when I open my eyes. Where am I? Squint. Someone else's room. Movie night. Is the movie over? It must be: Kimya Dawson's sweet voice is singing over the credits, "... and I'll say fuck Bush and fuck this war ..."

Blink. Is that a hand on my waist? What is it doing? What's—

I'm instantly awake. "The FUCK are you doing?!"

Ferguson is crouched at the foot of the bed, both hands tugging at the waistband of my black military-issued PT pants. He's already worked them halfway down my legs. Another hand is reaching for my underwear. Hamilton stands next to the bed, his uniform pants unbelted and unbuttoned. At the sound of my voice, they both freeze. I pull myself up and leap from the bed. "The FUCK!"

Yanking my pants back up, I fumble in the shadows for my shoes. My hand lands on my M16, sitting where I've left it at the end of the bed. I sling it over my shoulder, shoving its buttstock in the direction of Hamilton's groin as I shove my feet into my sneakers and bolt out the door. I stumble through the ankle-deep gravel, reaching my own door out of breath, and collapse into the folding chair next to our tiny stoop.

My brain, now on its spin cycle, generates alternating waves of confusion and rage. My heart pounds like an angry neighbor on the wall of my chest. I need a cigarette. I reach into my jacket pocket. It's empty. Fuck—I left my pack in Hamilton's room. Lighter, too.

Dammit, Self, echo the words in my head as I creep into my silent room. I collapse onto my bed. *Can't you do* any*thing right?* The springs creak obnoxiously as I land. My roommate stirs. "Roomie? That you?"

I sink into my pillow. In the not-so-distance, a mortar explodes. The last word that crosses my mind before sleep overtakes me is a soft, grateful, *safe*.

—

The Sonic Bomb's bed-shaking claxon jerks me back to disoriented consciousness. My duty hours have been switched back and forth from day to night shift so many times that whenever I wake up, it takes a few or more seconds to figure out whether the grey light filtering through my window is twilight or daybreak. This light, I blearily determine, is daytime—I went to bed at night. At night … but when? I don't remember going to bed. I bury my face in my pillow and let out a pained moan. My skull is on fire. I peel my sandpaper tongue from the roof of my mouth. What is that sour taste? Is it … lemon-lime?

The events of movie night come flooding back, a merciless invasion of shameful truth. My head spins as I attempt to sit up. The dizziness nearly knocks me back down to my pillow before I can grab the open doors of the wall locker next to my bed to steady myself. I can't tell if the sickness I feel in my stomach is from the liquor or the betrayal of my friends, but one thing is certain: I can't be late for work. Regret for my failure to see Hamilton and Ferguson as potential enemies will have to sink in later—I need all available energy to put on my uniform and walk through the headquarters to my office, straight past their desks, just like every other day.

—

"So, you're having trouble sleeping?" Doc Edmonds asks, ushering me into her plywood-walled, open-ceilinged office and closing the door.

"Yeah ..." I hesitate. I know she won't ask for more details. The doc and I have a hometown in common, and we've developed a rapport over the course of our fourteen months deployed together. She can tell I'm holding back. I hate to lie, but if I tell her what's keeping me awake at night, she'll have to report it. Then I'll have to try—and fail—to prove it. I'll have to relive it, and then I'll have to answer for breaking the rules. No, in this case, dishonesty is definitely the best policy.

"Are you eating regularly?" The major's face shows genuine concern, an unfamiliar look for most military personnel, especially those wearing her rank. Most of the uniformed women I know, even other officers, grow less agreeable with every promotion—a necessary show of dominance in this hyper-aggressive environment. Even from a doctor, visible empathy is unusual.

"Um ... I think I'm eating enough." *Once or twice a day counts as enough. Care-package Slim Jims are food, right?* "It's been too hot to go to the chow hall in the daytime." Temperatures are already stretching toward triple-digits and it's only halfway through April.

"It is pretty hot, huh?" She peers down at her notepad. "How about water? Staying hydrated?"

"I drink a liter of water every day."

She narrows her eyes admonishingly. "You really should be trying for two or three."

"I'll work on it, ma'am."

Another glance at the notepad. "Okay ... and what about exercise? Are you doing daily PT?"

"Yes ... well, most days." She doesn't need to know I've ceased and desisted voluntary exercise after passing my most recent PT test. In just a few weeks, when this deployment is over, I'll be done with the military, never again to need to care how many push-ups I can do in two minutes.

"All right ..." she scans her notes. "Well, what do you think is the problem?"

"Probably just stress, ma'am."

She nods and makes a note. "Everyone's under a lot of stress right now. Getting near the end of the deployment, people start to lose their bearing." It's true. We're almost done, but I haven't seen anyone in the headquarters smile in weeks. The doc looks back down at her notes, then back up with a sympathetic frown. "So, what do you want? Ambien? Ten? Twenty?"

"Thanks, ma'am. Twenty will be great."

She writes the script and hands it to me. "Get some sleep, okay? We're almost done. Home stretch."

"Roger, ma'am. I'll try."

"Come see me if you need a refill."

I thank her again and leave the tiny office, pulling the flimsy door shut behind me. Out of the corner of my eye, I can see Hamilton and Ferguson in their shared workspace across the narrow walkway, just fifty feet to my right. I can feel them staring in my direction as I turn left, toward my office, upstairs and out of sight.

My last interaction with them was expectedly uneasy. It was the next morning, a full week ago now. I'd decided to handle our inevitable encounter with the efficiency and professionalism of a strip-mall bikini wax. As I passed their desks, Hamilton had busied himself with a suddenly-urgent mission in the far corner of the office. I'd stopped and looked Ferguson in the face. "Do you have my cigarettes?" My tone was flat, polite, and unmistakably hostile.

Averting his eyes, he'd reached into his pocket and produced a slim, stainless-steel case that snugly held eight cigarettes and a lighter. I held out my hand and he dropped it into my palm. I slipped it into the cavernous cargo pocket of my uniform trousers with a terse, "Thank you." His mumbled "You're welcome" barely registered—before he'd opened his mouth, I was already at the other end of the building.

I've veered away from their vicinity ever since, speed-walking past their desks in the absence of an alternate entrance to the guarded building. That night they'd backed off in such a hurry that now I refuse to see them as a threat—especially not during the day, in the middle of the headquarters. But even while harmless, their presence is a nagging reminder of my own failure to see the danger in front of my face. The moment I step out of Doc Edmonds' office is my closest encounter with them in days, a testament to the breakneck stride I've cultivated to assist with my avoidance strategy.

At work, I deflect casual conversation from the newly-arrived replacement soldiers whose job description, till we clear out, appears to be "mill around office, hovering obnoxiously." I swivel absent-mindedly in my wobbly chair for a minute, idly letting my eyes dart in and out of focus as they scan the emails on the screen in front of me. Nothing important. All my tasks for the day is done, but that's how it always is by the middle of my shift, now that the division's getting ready to head back home. I'm mandated to stay in my place of duty until released, but there's one other option: the smoking area.

There's a secret smoking area on one side of the headquarters—secret, in that it isn't technically a smoking area, but can still be accessed from inside the building through a side door, and is tucked far enough away to be hidden from the view of power-tripping junior officers and NCOs. It's the closest thing I have to a fortress of solitude. The only other structures nearby are the generals' trailers, and those are surrounded by thirty-foot concrete blast walls. Every now and then, one of the three division commanders passes by as I'm slouching on one of the walls' ledges, scowling into the void as I use the end of my first cigarette to light the second. Even if I was conscientious enough to cower before rank, I wouldn't do so here—these generals all know me. I'm the soldier who constructs their daily newsletter, after all, and in this war, image is everything. My own NCOs barely know my first name, but the commanding general greets me by it. The secret smoking area is my safe space. Pulling the shiny stainless-steel case from my cargo pocket, I push the button to pop it open and flip a cigarette from its protective arm.

I bought the cigarette-holder in an effort to cut back on smoking, once I hit a pack a day. Its effectiveness is dampened by the presence of the carton I keep in my desk drawer but still, when empty, it at least serves as an encouraging reminder that I've smoked only eight delicious nicotine sticks, not twenty. I run my finger over the case's smooth surface, tracing the scratches it's incurred as a passenger in my pocket. Feeling an unexpected impression, I look down. There's an indentation on the case's front, where there was none before. It mars the mirror-like surface, an ugly scar on its previously clean countenance. An inch to the right and the jostle that created it might've damaged the latch's spring mechanism. For now though, functionality is intact. I double-check to confirm and breathe a rare sigh of relief. Just bruised. Not broken. Not this time.

ARMY DUMB

I chuckle to myself as I click Send and push my chair away from the desk. *Let them keep me tethered to this stupid newsletter for the whole deployment. They'll wish they'd let me out.* It's depressing enough to be spending an unknown amount of time in a war zone I'd thought I'd never see again. Spending that time doing a job that could have been accomplished anywhere in the world with an internet connection feels more like a daily insult than gainful employment. My official Army job title is the simultaneously pretentious and oxymoronic "print journalist/public affairs specialist," but starting today, my soul is pure civilian.

Standing up for a long-needed stretch, I glance at the calendar: June 12, 2007. I poke my head over the short cubicle wall between Staff Sergeant Gonzalez and me.

"Hey Sergeant, guess what today is?" He looks up from his computer screen expectantly. "It's my ETS day! Congratulate me!"

He snorts. "Congratulations. I guess we know why they call it an *estimated* time of separation date."

"I don't even care if we have a year left. They can keep my body here, but my mind is out of the Army, starting today."

"Ha! Was your mind ever in the Army to begin with?"

"Oh, whatever." He raises an eyebrow. I snort. "Hey, I know it's obvious I never wanted to be a soldier. I just didn't think they'd keep me in after the end of my contract."

"Welcome to the stop-loss club."

"And I especially didn't think they'd send me on another deployment just to sit here for twelve hours every night and make a stupid four-page newsletter that I could make from my bed at home."

"Come on—it's the Army. When does it ever make sense?"

I grimace. "Never. That's why I'm celebrating my last day in the military today anyway, even if I do still have to be here another year."

"Celebrating how? With sparkling grape juice and near-beer at the DFAC?"

"Nah, the dining facility is too far to walk in this heat. My celebration is more gratifying than that."

"Don't tell me about it. Whatever it is, I don't want anyone to think I'm in on it."

"Har, har. It's nothing illegal or against regulation." His face is undisguised skepticism. "Fine, don't believe me."

"Good luck."

Slinging my M16 over my shoulder, I pull my patrol cap off the weapons rack and flip him a parting wave. "I'm sure it'll be fine. All in good fun. See you tonight." After all these months working nights, I've finally gotten out of the habit of calling the next shift "tomorrow." Every day feels like a continuation of the next. At least now I have something to look forward to when I get back to the office in twelve hours. It isn't the finest mischief I've ever made, but it'll get the job done.

We've been in Iraq for three months, and word has just come down from the top that this deployment is going to last an additional year. The only information we were given before leaving home was that unlike the normal, year-long rotations, this one would be "a year to eighteen months." Now it seems someone in the upper echelons has finally decided to split the difference. But along with the relief of knowing my second tour will end three months before its longest possible duration, comes the phantom back-stab of remembering I still won't be getting out of the Army until nearly a year after my original active-duty contract should have expired—as it was set to do today. Instead of burning my uniforms and toasting my freedom, I'm here in Baghdad, wearing my disdain like a tattered badge of honor.

—

Intimately aware of the drastic repercussions for out-and-out revolt, I've swiveled my sights in the familiar direction of subtle rebellion. The delicate dance of expressing my displeasure while also staying out of trouble requires more finesse than I usually can claim. I've never shied away from sharing my opinions, but I'm not brave enough to risk the military's retaliation for real subversiveness. Still, I've done the research and discovered to my delight that there is no punitive action designated for simply annoying one's superior officers. There are dozens of ways to accomplish this goal, and with a year to eighteen months tacked onto my active-duty contract, I have nothing but time to explore them. It is, I've decided, a sign: if the Army won't let me out, I am certainly destined to be a pain in its ass.

"You know, you could just play their game," one of my fellow public affairs soldiers suggested while we were still stateside. Still relatively new to the military, she'd been brimming with enthusiasm to get over to Iraq and soldier around. "It's not that hard."

"Sure, it's easy to play the game, till the rules randomly change," I'd griped. "Let me know how you feel about it when your first-line supervisor claims you're on some mysterious 'do-not-retain' list that he can't produce."

"A do-not-retain list? What? Is that a real thing?"

"Probably not. But that's the excuse they're using to keep me from re-upping."

"Well … maybe it's real."

"If I can't reenlist, I'll be deployed. You really think I'd be on a list that makes me 'unretainable' but still deployable?"

"Well … hm. What's wrong with deploying?"

"Ugh, the last deployment almost drove me nuts."

"Yeah, I don't know what to tell you, dude. Doesn't seem like there's anything you can do about it, though."

"That's the only thing I definitely know is true. But hey, on the bright side, if they're this desperate to keep me in, there's probably nothing I can do that'll get me kicked out."

"That's the spirit!"

———

June on a military base in central Iraq is an unforgiving month, when dust and heat join forces to cripple lungs and critically injure morale. After a fitful day attempting to sleep in the sweltering thirty-person tent I refuse to call home, I stumble back through the shin-deep gravel blanketing our temporary neighborhood to work my night shift at Task Force Baghdad headquarters. Pallets of shrink-wrapped one-liter water bottles sink into the rocks and dirt, sweating beside the towering concrete blast walls that surround our tents.

I remind myself not to grab a bottle from one of the pallets that was sitting in the sun's hundred-three-degree heat all day while I slept. I've made that mistake before, burning my fingertips on its warped plastic, feeling like a true genius. "Army Dumb," an homage to our branch's new "Army Strong" motto, is the term some of us have taken to using for that slow decline of brain cells that kicks in while sucking it up and driving on. It's my firm belief that Army Dumb was responsible for the frying of my ass on a sun-baked portable toilet, as well as for the beginning and end of my marriage, and for my failure, last fall, to recognize what I should have suspected to be a conspiratorial plot to keep me from re-enlisting. I resist the urge to become cranky.

A few short minutes later, I'm at my desk, opening emails and enjoying a rare twinge of happiness at the results of my tiny gesture of rebellion. The first response I click on has a satisfyingly peeved tone. My button-pushing instinct was right.

It's from a major I've never met, and his indignation is palpable: "Specialist, I don't know who you are, but if this is your idea of a joke, it's not funny." I snort. *Yes, it is.* "This is an official military email server, not to be used for your personal opinions." A loud laugh escapes my throat before I can stop it. "I've CC'ed your OIC on this email and expect a change to be made immediately." *Wow, straight to the officer in charge. Slow day, sir?*

I can't imagine what he thinks my OIC's response will be. The lieutenant colonel, for all his superior rank, has been going to great lengths to avoid any kind of confrontation with me ever since he banned me from writing op-eds and obstructed my attempt to flee his leadership. I can't imagine *this* will be the minor offense that will send him scurrying to discipline me.

The next email proves my theory wrong: while still avoiding face-to-face interaction, the colonel is making his stand.

"Specialist, you know what this is regarding. Change it immediately." I sigh. *These officers have no sense of humor.* No matter. This game has a second level.

"I'm sorry, sir," I type back. "I'm not sure I understand the problem. Change what, exactly?"

The reply from three cubicles to my right comes swiftly. "Your signature block. Change it now." I smile. If he insists.

"Roger, sir." *Send.* Clicking over to the signature block settings, I highlight the quote placed one line below my name, rank, and position:

> *"America ... just a nation of two hundred million used car salesmen with all the money we need to buy guns and no qualms about killing anybody else in the world who tries to make us uncomfortable."*

> — Hunter S. Thompson

In only one day, it has done its work well. Time to move on. I open a document I've prepared for this eventuality, copy the top few lines of text, and replace the offending quote with a new one:

> *"I mean no harm nor put fault*
> *On anyone that lives in a vault*
> *But it's alright, Ma, if I can't please him."*

> — Bob Dylan

This new game is a rare silver lining on the dark cloud of my present position. Tasked with assembling a daily newsletter lauding the heroics of the troops, I'm also required to email a digital version of the publication to all of Task Force Baghdad's unit commanders, who then feed it to their soldiers. As long as I have the eye of the top brass, I've decided, I ought to use the opportunity to pass on some under-appreciated literary gems. "What are they going to do—stop-loss me and send me to Iraq?" has become my mantra. I'm not overtly challenging anyone's authority, but my point is clear: if I must be here on your terms, you must put up with me. It isn't the path of least resistance, but now that they've forced me back into their war, I can't resist pulling them into my own battle of wills.

The alleged "do-not-retain list" is what pushed me over the edge. I was never convinced of the list's existence. If there was a blanket stop-loss order in place, the Army clearly couldn't afford to not-retain soldiers—but every person in my chain of command assured me that this list was real, and that I was on it. It was the only thing standing in the way of freedom—not only from stop-loss, but from a year in a combat zone with people who are, beyond all doubts, completely full of shit.

———

Sitting in my childhood bedroom five and a half years ago, reading my enlistment contract, I was confused about the part in small print that referred to this being an eight-year contract. *But I'm only signing up for five.* When I asked my recruiter about it, he said not to worry. "That just means when you get out after five years, you're part of the Inactive Ready Reserve for another three," he said. "It's not active duty unless you're called back—but don't worry about that. It probably won't happen. Here, have we talked about the college money yet?"

I didn't give it another thought until two years in, when, in the midst of open-ended wars in Iraq and Afghanistan, the military issued the stop-loss/stop-movement order to keep the Army from hemorrhaging personnel. The effects of what we all call the "back-door draft" reverberated throughout our ranks, and morale plunged to new depths. The topic got so hot that I was assigned to write an op-ed about it for the post newspaper. I grappled with the headline for hours, finally settling on "Stop-Loss: A Necessary Evil, or Just Necessary?" *Or Just Evil,* I'd mentally revised.

The consensus among the other troops I interviewed was that stop-loss was a big steaming pile of fuckery as far as their lives were concerned, but a steaming pile for which they begrudgingly acknowledged they'd unwittingly volunteered. None of us had heard of stop-loss before the policy went into effect, but we've all known since Basic Training that once we're given orders, all we can legally do is follow them.

———

Everyone in the headquarters works twelve-hour shifts during deployment. It takes me two to three hours to complete my job each night, which means I have a dangerous number of remaining hours to entertain myself before I'm allowed to leave. Staggered shifts mean there are always sad-eyed soldiers occupying dreary cubes and makeshift plywood-walled offices throughout the night, hunched over dust-covered laptop screens or sprawled like marionettes in their tiny-wheeled office chairs, not caring who might see them sleep.

One of my favorite ways to avoid any unintended productivity that might result from staying at my desk is a technique I call the walkabout: wandering around the headquarters, I pay short visits to all my friends in their respective sections, always staying slightly ahead of any officer or NCO from my own section who might come looking for me. My job as a public affairs specialist requires me to be at least passingly acquainted with personnel from every section, so I can stretch this game out for as many hours as necessary—and many hours are necessary. One night, I happened by the Personnel section, where a few bored junior-enlistees were printing themselves custom ID badges. Ten short minutes later, I was the proud owner of a brand-new badge depicting my winking face, pointing at the camera with a toothy grin. It made everyone laugh, so I took to wearing it on my uniform blouse, under my security badge—"for morale purposes," I explained to the division command sergeant major, who happened to be passing by one night while I was flipping up the top badge to give my fellow troops a chuckle.

"Morale, huh? Let me see what you got there, soldier." I showed him. He let out a snort before he could stop himself. "Well. That's pretty funny, soldier."

"Roger, Sergeant Major!" He wagged his head as though to shake away the smile trying to appear on it.

"Carry on, soldier!"

The next morning before ending my shift, I was called down to the front of the headquarters to take a group photo of the command team with a visiting official. The division command sergeant major had the glossy-eyed face of early-morning meetings, and as I framed the shot, I caught his eye. "Smile, Sergeant Major!"

He snorted. "Just take the picture, soldier."

I flipped my security badge up, and at the surprise sight of my wink, his stoic expression broke into a wide grin. I snapped the photo and held my breath, waiting for the rebuke that had to be coming.

Instead, he laughed, and a ritual was established: each time I showed up to take a photo of the sergeant major, I'd flip up my badge a second before pressing the shutter down. And in every photo, his smile was the biggest.

———

It was during my evening wanderings that I found myself in the battalion retention office a few weeks ago, discussing the finer points of early-'90s pop music with Staff Sergeant Colfax as he worked late organizing reenlistment bonus gifts into a precarious pile in the corner. I caught a glimpse of something shiny peeking out of one of the boxes.

"Are those … flasks?"

"Yeah. Nice ones, too. Stainless steel, with the division logo on them."

"I want one!"

"Reenlist and you'll get one."

I snorted bitterly.

"Don't even talk to me about reenlisting."

"Hey, it's my job. I have to try."

"Wouldn't do you any good even if I wanted to."

"Why do you say that?"

"I already tried to reenlist back in October, before stop-loss went into effect. It didn't work."

"What do you mean, it didn't work?" His brow crinkled. "How could it not work? What happened?"

"Have you ever heard of a do-not-retain list?" His eyebrows furrowed.

"Uh … no. A do-not-retain list?"

"Yeah, you know, like, to keep people from reenlisting if they've gotten too many negative counseling statements?"

"Uh, I mean, I've heard of flags on reenlistment, but that's for specific reasons. Like for being overweight, or failing too many PT tests, or refusing to be promoted. That's pretty much it."

"But, not a list of soldiers who are just flat-out unretainable."

"No. That would be ridiculous."

I sighed. Confirmation. "Tell that to my chain of command."

His eyes widened. "Your chain of command told you that you were on a do-not-retain list?"

"Roger that."

He shook his head, as though the motion would make the pieces of this puzzle fall into place. "Why would they do that?"

"I was trying to reenlist for a different duty station so I wouldn't have to deploy with them. They didn't want to have to get a replacement for me so …"

"So they told you some bullshit about a do-not-retain list."

"Roger."

He clicked his tongue. "That's fucked up."

"Oh, I know."

"Because, you know, you could have reenlisted."

"Yeah. I figured as much."

"Like, any time."

"Thanks."

"But instead …"

"Instead, I'm here."

He let out a low whistle. "Damn. You should've come and talked to me."

"I didn't know you then! Anyway, that's why I'm not going to reenlist. As soon as this deployment is done, I'm getting the fuck out of the Army and never coming back."

He'd stopped his organization process and sat back on his heels, staring at the boxes in front of him. Leaning suddenly forward, he reached into one of them, pulled out a plastic-wrapped something, and tossed it underhand to me. I caught it. "What's this?"

"Your reenlistment gift." It was heavy. Metal. I turned it over. Through the plastic wrapping I could see the 3rd Infantry Division logo.

"Aw. You're giving me a flask?"

He nodded.

"Even though I'm not re-upping?"

"Don't tell anyone."

"I won't. But, why?"

He sighed. "Because you're going to need it."

—

It's ten p.m., three hours into my shift. The last of the NCOs has just left. The officers disappeared hours ago, and my first-line supervisor is off somewhere with his other soldier, whose company and existence he openly prefers. I reach into the discreet ankle pocket of my uniform trousers and pull out the heavy object weighing down my right side. Checking the nearly-emptied offices in the room for nosy stragglers, I duck out of sight, behind the half-walls of my back-corner work area.

Unscrewing the flask, I tip a discreet stream of Johnnie Walker Red into my mouth, savoring the burn as it trickles down my throat, silently thanking the civilian contractor who smuggled the whiskey in from the Green Zone and generously shared it with me. This has become as regular a coping mechanism as I can manage, depending on my source's reliability. I've done the math and decided it's worth the risk of faint booze-breath to feel that warm, enveloping blanket of fuck-it-all envelop my frenzied mind as the hours creep past.

Tonight is my last night shift of the deployment, and I'm making it count—at least, making it count in a way that won't delay my departure date from this all-too familiar war zone. I'm using, for one last time, the only weapon at my disposal that can't be used against me: other people's words. I've learned by now that thanks to the filter-removing effects of insomnia, my own words can't be trusted to keep my life from getting harder—unless I count last week's nervous breakdown. Screaming at my NCO that this was ALL. FUCKING. BULLSHIT has led to the pleasant new development of my superiors leaving me as entirely alone as possible, giving me plenty of time to contemplate the mess I've been in for the past six years.

The mission I chose to accept as a naive nineteen-year-old has grown, like the deployment itself, less bearable the better I've gotten to know it. My job is officially to "tell the Army's story" of the coalition's victorious liberation of Iraq. After two trips to Baghdad, where the U.S. is "fighting" its enemies by throwing money and weapons at certain militias and tribes while confiscating it from others, I'm finding it increasingly challenging to see anything victorious about the Army's story, or anything liberated about the Iraqis.

Every time I visit a neighborhood or rural community to document its (dubitable) safety and (minimal) services, the only local residents I see in a remotely unsuspicious mood are young children and members of the newly-minted Iraqi security forces. The U.S.-led occupation (or "reconstruction," depending on which media outlet is talking about it) is in its fifth year, and still there's no sign of regular electricity, water, sewage treatment, healthcare, or education for millions of Iraqis, despite the gallons of dollars gushing out of the Department of Defense into the waiting hands of military contractors, ostensibly for this purpose.

On Camp Victory, expressions are undeniably grim. I'm one of many who've been stop-lossed, as it's come to be verbed, but by our fourteenth month in-country, even those who knew they'd deploy all along wear scowls more or less permanently affixed to their faces. The only sincere smile I've seen in months was on the recently-promoted Sergeant Mele, an old buddy from my first deployment. I bumped directly into him on my way to cover a joint Iraqi-U.S. patrol out of Forward Operating Base Falcon. When he recognized me, he grinned. "Dude!"

"Mele! Been a long time!"

"Like two years, right? Dude, but I'm finally working in my job! No more fuckin' headquarters hell!"

"Nice! No more desk job!"

"Fuck no. Now I go out on patrol every day like I'm supposed to."

We worked in the headquarters together for the full year of our first deployment, and complained together over many a smoke break. He was trained as a combat engineer, but had then been stuck in admin due to a personnel shortage in admin and an over-abundance of combat engineers. *Typical soldier—he's happier the more danger he's in*, I caught myself thinking smirkily, before remembering I wouldn't be talking to him if I, too, hadn't been aching to escape the headquarters' relatively-safe monotony (not counting sporadic explosions of indirect fire), along with its excessive population of generals and officers who wanted to be generals.

Mele's smile was infectious. He always was an upbeat kind of guy. I'd forgotten. Headquarters had a way of sucking the upbeat right out of a person. I couldn't help but return his grin.

"Well shit, dude, it's great you're happy."

"You know? I really am."

We caught up a bit more before we both had other places to be: he was still married, he told me with understandable relief, with a step-daughter just graduated from preschool. I told him about my impending divorce and shady stop-loss situation. He shook his head.

"Man, they really fucked you."

"Don't I know it."

"Well, it *is* the Army way."

"Yup. We all get fucked some way, somehow."

"Right in the ass. I'm just glad it's not happening to me right now."

We said our goodbyes and I headed off to meet up with the unit I was joining on patrol that afternoon. Other than a few minor details, I already knew what my article would say. The headline would be simple: 'US-Iraqi joint patrol keeps [name of Baghdad neighborhood] safe.' I'd include quotes from soldiers and Iraqi police about how well the mission was going, snap a few photos of everyone in uniform interacting with the locals, and come up with as many ways as possible to say nothing about the apparent ineptitude of the Iraqi security forces, made up entirely of poor farmers and villagers with no better options. I knew better by now than to even allude to the general concept of failure in print since the chief of staff had expressly forbidden use of the word, but still—everywhere I look, there's failure.

As far as I can tell, five years after the "surgical" airstrikes flashily-nicknamed "Shock and Awe" leveled the nation's cities, government, and infrastructure, our presence in Iraq is a clear indicator that if an exit strategy ever existed here, it has to have gone horribly awry. Either that, or—I shudder at the thought that I don't want to believe—this whole debacle could be intentional. We might have made a huge mess here, but ... we got the evil dictator out, right? I'm woefully uneducated when it comes to foreign policy, but everything I've absorbed throughout my short life has told me that evil dictators must be toppled, and the U.S.A. is the good guy.

The Army calls me a journalist, but by the time I finish writing what I'm told, I don't have enough investigative energy left to ask the one question that's been bubbling beneath my consciousness: if U.S. soldiers are the good guys—heroes, even!—but the military still treats us like disposable property, why would anyone who *isn't* us in this country be treated any better? Civilian reporters compare the conflict in Iraq to Vietnam, and all I have to do is look around to see they must be right. But surely that's only an unfortunate accident, I tell myself, one nobody could have seen coming. True, our current mission looks a lot more like damage control than like any kind of intentional plan ... but would the generals really have agreed to invade Iraq, costing the lives of thousands of U.S. soldiers and potentially millions of Iraqi civilians, without at least *believing* those lives wouldn't be lost in vain? Watching Baghdad pass by through Humvee windows, I keep an eye out for roadside bombs and suspicious characters, up to and including children, and try not to hear the voice in the back of my mind gently whispering the answer I don't want to acknowledge.

The truth finally pushes its way through my mental barricades a few weeks later. It's a week after my birthday, and I'm in better spirits than usual after receiving care packages containing cartons of cigarettes that weren't all stale, like the ones at the post exchange. On my way out of the headquarters to the smoking area, I'm nearly toppled by a soldier hurrying into the building with his head pointed non-tactically downward.

"Hey, watch where you're going!" I blurt without thinking, crossing my fingers that I haven't just admonished an officer or NCO, either of whom would feel entitled to not only bowl over junior-enlisted soldiers, but blame us for it. Luckily, when he turns around to mumble an apology, I see the down-turned face is a familiar one—another admin lackey who enlisted as an engineer but found himself stuck in the headquarters.

"Stack! What's up? You almost knocked me over!"

"Hey dude, I'm sorry. I wasn't looking where I was going." Now that I can see his face, I notice his typical expression of annoyance is gone, replaced with one of ... sadness? I haven't seen a fully-re-alized emotion other than rage or disgust in months so can't be sure, but I figure it has to be either that or constipation.

"Are you okay?" *Is that a tear in his eye?*

"Oh, dude. You haven't heard."

"Heard what?" He motions me out of the doorway and back into the headquarters. I follow him to a quiet corner just past the front doors. On one of the walls hangs a sixty-inch LCD mon-itor. The commanding general has designated it for the explicit purpose of displaying a slide show featuring names, photos, and pertinent details of every soldier who's been killed in action during this deployment. Usually there are at least a few soldiers milling around the area, either staring solemnly at the screen or casually ignoring it, but today it's empty except for Stack and me. He takes a deep breath and meets my eyes.

"It's Mele."

"Oh fuck. No ..."

"He's dead."

"FUCK."

"An IED."

"Goddammit." An improvised explosive device, one of the ubiq-uitous enemy's preferred weapons. I feel the lump in my throat rise before I could stop it. *There's no crying in the headquarters.* Before the tears can pour, I choke them back, instead emitting a second, more forceful, "GODDAMMIT!"

"Yeah dude, I know."

"FUCK! I just saw him a few weeks ago at FOB Falcon!"

"It happened last week." Reflexively, my head turns to the screen on the wall next to us, where faces, names, birth and death dates scroll on a perpetual loop—I can't believe it's true until I see that official photo in front of me, dates perfectly aligned beside it, all hovering above the animated American flag waving patrioti-cally in the background. Stack catches the direction of my gaze. "He's not up there yet."

I refuse to let the tears emerge. "This is bullshit."

"I know, dude. I know. He was my best friend. We just bought houses on the same street."

"Fuuuuuck."

Heaving a sigh, he straightens his back. "I gotta get to work. I'll let you know when they're doing the memorial service."

"All right, buddy. Thanks for telling me."

"Yeah. Of course."

My feet feel nailed to the floor. I stare blank-eyed at the screen, still flipping through slide after slide bearing face after face of dead soldiers, dead battle buddies, dead best friends. Dead teenagers. *What is the fucking point of this? What. Is. The fucking. Point? Nobody is winning here.*

———

Days away from my final flight home, I'm still wrestling with all the probable causes for this war floating through my mental ether: *Money. Oil. Power. Strategy.* Every night, for fourteen consecutive months, I've produced four pages of full-color victory, lauding the accomplishments of coalition troops even as the casualty count continues to climb. During my first deployment two years ago, nearly eight-hundred and fifty U.S. soldiers lost their lives in twelve months, in addition to the vast numbers of Iraqi deaths we aren't officially counting. This time, in one year, more than nine hundred bodies have already been shipped back to the States in flag-covered coffins that the media aren't allowed to photograph.

This war in Iraq was touted to the American people as a lib-eration mission, but sitting at my desk, preparing to send my final email with the final newsletter to every Task Force Baghdad commander from the coalition commander on down, all I can think is, *Who has been liberated here?* Not the Iraqis, still living under a corrupt government but now controlled, for all intents and purposes, by the United States, with no clean water, competent security, or reliable electricity. Not the people of the United States, whose hard-earned dollars are being dumped like garbage into defense contracts. Not us soldiers, especially those of us here involuntarily. Not the thousands of remittance laborers from the Philippines brought in to work here three years at a time for a pittance to send home to their families. When I look around the base where I've spent more than two of my past four years of life, I see miserable faces. When I leave the base and go into the city, I see fearful faces. When I watch the news, I see angry faces. Even the highly-paid contractors, the Blackwater mercenaries who bounce from mission to nefarious mission in ominous black helicopters, are rarely seen without a scowl on their dark-sunglassed countenances.

Nobody has been liberated here. We're all prisoners of this war. The stark realization sinks into my consciousness like a lead weight. Nobody is winning the war, yet on it rages, billions of tax dollars deep already, filling the pockets of politicians and defense contractors as the well-intentioned bodies of broken soldiers and civilian bystanders pile up. *My friends are dying for the cause of more death.*

Like so many of my fellow enlistees, I joined the Army for job training, college money, and adventure—but others, like Mele, signed up with the simple desire to be of service to their country. They never suspected that desire would be manipulated, and their lives given up as collateral damage in what was looking more and more like a perpetually-raging power struggle.

Time to refocus on the task at hand. Turning to face my computer screen, I click Send to beam the last newsletter of my six-year military career into the ether, and bid it good riddance. *This is the last time I will use my mind to produce deception. No more of this.*

The body of my email is short, bearing the same words it does every day: "Dear Sir, attached is today's edition of the *Dog Face Daily*." Beneath it, my name, rank and title. And under that, in an obnoxiously large font, a song that has been running relentlessly through my head.

> *"Far between sundown's finish an' midnight's broken toll*
>
> *We ducked inside the doorway, thunder crashing*
>
> *As majestic bells of bolts struck shadows in the sounds*
>
> *Seeming to be the chimes of freedom flashing*
>
> *Flashing for the warriors whose strength is not to fight*
>
> *Flashing for the refugees on the unarmed road of flight*
>
> *An' for each an' ev'ry underdog soldier in the night*
>
> *An' we gazed upon the chimes of freedom flashing.'*
>
> — Bob Dylan, 'Chimes of Freedom'"

I close my laptop, sling my weapon over my shoulder, and wave goodbye to Sergeant Gonzalez. Pushing the headquarters' double doors open for the last time, I breathe a sigh of relief. The harsh light of the morning sun floods my eyes, but all I can see are the chimes of freedom, flashing.

FLASHBACKS

"What are you doing right now, Specialist?"

"Just laying out the newspaper, Sergeant."

"Put that down for now. I need you to escort a reporter to talk to some soldiers."

"Roger that."

"Here's a list of talking points. Don't forget to keep it simple, so they can remember."

"Of course. Where's the reporter from?"

"Fox. He's a friendly. Just make sure nobody says anything stupid."

"Roger, Sergeant."

We never thought it would be necessary to closely supervise the media around soldiers who had no classified or sensitive information to accidentally leak. Then some dumb private, on a long gate-guard shift outside the headquarters, decided to complain to a wandering writer from one of the major publications—some kind of tirade about redundancy and the general feeling of futility the rest of us knew not to mention to the press. The offending reporter had, of course, lost her access to the troops, but the Army's truth-blood had been drawn. We had to work quickly to mitigate any ripple of excitement this unauthorized burst of honesty might create in the hearts of civilian journalists—or, as the rest of the world knew them, journalists.

We call ourselves "military journalists," not because it's accurate, but because that's what we've been trained to call ourselves. It's our job to help the civilian journalists write only what we want them to write. On the rare occasions our work comes into inconvenient contact with the notion that what we're doing is the exact opposite of journalism, I simply remind myself that we are soldiers first, and thus not responsible for the paradox inherent in the joint job titles of "journalist" and "public affairs specialist."

Knowing I'm just doing my job doesn't make me feel any less dirty for doing it. *You should be glad*, I chastise myself. *You're not stuck behind a desk on night shift again, compiling the* real *journalists' articles into a searchable format for the general.* At least in my current position, I can *almost* sleep at night. Theoretically, anyway. In practice, it's more like lying wide awake in the dark, wishing I'd ignored the recruiter's call, wondering why I didn't just wait till I could afford to finish school.

———

"So what am I supposed to say, again?"

I sigh. Coaching soldiers on how to talk to the press is a task well-suited for one of the inner circles of hell.

"You have confidence in your leaders and believe the mission will be a success."

"Okay. I think I can remember that."

"Repeat it back to me."

"I'm confident in your leaders and believe the mission will be a success."

"No, you're confident in *your* leaders."

"Oh, yeah. I'm confident in *my* leaders and believe the mission will be a success."

"Great. You got it. Do you remember the first part?"

"Uhhh ..."

"You've seen the work of the Iraqi security forces ..."

"Oh, haha. Right. I've seen the work of the Iraqi security forces and believe they're doing a great job—hey, do I have to mean this?"

"Well ..."

"Because for real, they're tore up."

"Shh!" I look around to make sure the reporter is out of earshot. "Yeah ... I know. Can you say you've, maybe, seen improvement in the ISF?"

"I mean, I guess that would technically be true. They've improved, like, a little."

"Okay, let's go with that, then. You've seen improvement in the Iraqi security forces and believe they're doing a great job."

"They're doing an okay job."

You're killing me, bud. "All right ... they're doing their best with a difficult situation?"

"Uh, I don't know. I hope it's not their best."

"They're doing better as time goes on?"

"I guess."

"Perfect. Say that. I'll send the reporter in."

It could be worse, I reassure myself. I could have enlisted for a psychological operations job, where I'd *really* be messing with people's heads. This is just a bit of light truth-bending to boost morale. Nobody wants the soldiers getting depressed in the middle of a war.

And we can't have the people back home thinking of us as the bad guys. The government learned its lesson during the Vietnam War, when the televised sight of burning bodies and shell-shocked villagers fueled national outcry over the injustice of it all. That won't be happening this time around. This time, the war has talking points.

———

When people back home ask what kind of news I'm writing, I usually keep my answer as simple as possible. "I write the Army's news," I tell them with a pleasant-yet-dismissive smile. If they press the matter, I ask them if they ever read the regular news about the war. "Yes? Well, I write the opposite of that." If some well-meaning friend or relative pushes me to elaborate, I break it down: "Look, if you really want to get an idea of how things are going in Iraq, read our articles after you read the newspaper. They'll give you only the bad news, we'll give you only the good news, and you'll kind of end up with the full story."

"Oh," they nod, backing slowly away. "I see."

But, of course, they can't see. Neither can I, really.

———

It's 2011. I've been out of the Army for three years. I'm sitting in a classroom at the school where I've decided to spend the first half of my GI Bill—the University of California at Berkeley—and I'm beginning to understand why we went to such great lengths to trick our fellow troops into thinking we were not only winning the war, but heroes for waging it in the first place.

The course is Political Science 142: Economics, Politics and Ideas in the Middle East and North Africa. I'm taking it on the way to my bachelor's degree in "Near Eastern Studies," and am eager to crack the surface of everything I don't know. This is my first time studying anywhere I've occupied as part of an invading force.

When we reach the part of the syllabus headed "The Iraq War" in bold, I feel an unfamiliar tension in my chest. I studied U.S. wars in school as a kid, but now it's been less than five years since my first deployment, and here I am, watching my head try to wrap itself around the idea that the war I was in has somehow become part of the past, while I still think of it in the present tense. My friends are still fighting it, after all. Sometimes I wonder if I am, too.

"So, where were you on 9/11?" I ask the other members of my study group, as we go over the stated justifications for use of military force in Iraq. We've made a list: the threat of Arab terrorists, the fear of angry Muslims, the parallel insistence that Saddam had weapons of mass destruction that tied the two ideas inextricably together.

I was in community college that day, I tell them. In a U.S. history class. I remember it well. The morning everything changed.

They shift in their chairs. "I was in third grade," one of my classmates finally offers.

"I was in fourth," says another.

"I was in middle school," says the lone senior in the group. They all look at me sheepishly as I do the mental math.

On average, they're a decade younger than my twenty-nine years. They're some of the brightest minds of a generation that's grown up in the shadow of the "War on Terror," never knowing a different world. Now, together, we're learning all the ways the post-9/11 backlash against generically-Arab "jihadists" was inflated by our own government and used to conflate Iraq with terrorism. Together, we read in black and white that there was never any confirmation of weapons of mass destruction in Saddam Hussein's arsenal—that the media was fed that story by government officials and, in turn, fed it to the American people. Together, we take notes on the research that shows how the Iraq War was fought with, yes, bombs and ammunition, but also with strategically-controlled information.

"Did you write down the part with the official line about winning hearts and minds?" one of my classmates asks, head hunched over his notebook.

I nod, holding back the response that leaps first to my tongue: *I don't need to.* After all the times I had to write it, that line is seared into my brain like a brand.

Together, we learn about the hidden-in-plain-sight context of the war, the history none of us know about Western control of Iraq, and the power balance that was so tenuously struck there until March of 2003, when its U.S.-propped dictator refused to continue cooperating with his puppeteers. We watch clips of George W. Bush admitting there were no WMDs *or* ties to 9/11 in Iraq. We go slightly further back in history and review the national boundaries the British and French drew to divide up the Middle East in the 1916 Sykes-Picot agreement.

It's already begun to dawn on me that the stories of "thousands of years of conflict" in the Middle East were an exaggeration, but I don't have to dig much deeper to discover how and why I was led to believe they were true at all: we in the U.S. just weren't ready to support out-and-out regime change in Iraq unless we could call ourselves liberators.

I can't help but laugh at my soldier-self—I enlisted to get trained as a journalist, but didn't even do the minimal investigation I would have needed to understand why my job was to with-hold news, not spread it. I was so caught up in the idea of a grand educational adventure in the military that I missed the lesson I should have learned from the moment my recruiter told me to hide my history of asthma from the doctor at my first physical: not only does the government lie to soldiers, but it expects us all to lie on its behalf.

———

"Perception is reality, soldier," one of my sergeants used to sneer derisively. He meant it as a way of threatening reprisal for my refusal to act like I believed in the public affairs mission. "Perception is reality": I heard it as the mission, encapsulated. If we restrict every type of perception except one, we create our own version of reality.

What if I'd told the recruiter I wasn't interested? The question takes up residence in the back of my mind while my study group continues its discussion around me. I hear myself participating, even as my thoughts stray. Maybe if I'd stuck it out in community college—gotten financial aid, gone to a real journalism school—I would have eventually become one of the reporters looking for the truth about the war from soldiers trained to hide it from them. I want to believe I'd have been one of the independent types, seeking out the true story at any cost.

Maybe I would have gone to any lengths to find the answers being kept from me. Or maybe I, too, would have simply stuck to the script and written down the talking points, knowing they'd been carefully crafted to communicate nonexistent victory, and unwilling to challenge them for fear of losing my status as Approved Press. Maybe I still would have listened to official lines channeled through the mouths of scowling, sunburned soldiers, and maybe I'd have heard their spoon-fed lies as truth, desperately wanting to believe my perception could be reality.

But I didn't do any of that. Instead, I took an oath to protect and defend the United States Constitution, then promptly received orders that violated it. Now, in a crowded lecture hall, I'm surrounded by adults who were children when I swore my enlistment oath. The soldier-filter that was fitted firmly over my field of vision has fallen away, a student-lens dropping into its place. My perceptions have shifted, and with them, my reality.

I remember my recruiter's voice, full of confidence as he assured me my nearsightedness wouldn't be a problem. The waiver would come through, he'd said, as long as there was no way for me to claim the Army had made me blind. My eyes have undoubtedly worsened since I took my oath of enlistment, and the vision I had for my life has been blurred, yes—but blind? No. The Army didn't make me blind. My sight is the clearest it's ever been.

ACKNOWLEDGMENTS

There's a part of me that wants to start this section by acknowledging the name of every politician who's voted to fund military recruitment instead of universal healthcare, or chosen to send teenagers to war instead of college. I don't want to waste energy on murderers and warmongers, though, so rather than list most of the members of every past and current legislative and executive branch of government, I'll just say that this book shouldn't have to exist, but because of them, I had to write it. I have no choice but to acknowledge the powers-that-be who profit by using taxes to train children to kill strangers, instead of to help us all live for and with each other. Without them, I might have gone to school, instead of war, during my formative years. But here we are, and there they go. I wish I could trade them all away to get my dear friends back who were lost in the wars they waged, to bring back all the civilian lives lost as "collateral damage," to reclaim the 22 veterans a day who choose suicide over a life spent suffering the perpetual pain of post-traumatic stress and moral injury—but I can't. All I can do is try, in my own clumsy way, to keep raging against the machine that's intent on destroying us, by telling the stories of the souls it has stolen.

Beyond that, it's hard to know where to begin. The flood of faces that rushes through my brain as I face this page is best represented not by a list of names, but as a sea of emotions, speckled with blurry versions of familiar images and distorted snippets of intimate conversations. If I mistakenly leave anyone out here, I promise it's due more to my aging brain than to any ill will, and offer my apologies to anyone who might take offense.

First, to you, the reader of these words: I am deeply grateful for the time and energy you've invested in reading this book. Thank you so much for hearing these stories, no matter how difficult they are to digest, and for giving me the gift of your precious attention. I especially want to give gratitude to ...

... everyone who's even briefly mentioned in these pages, who lived these stories with me, who directly or inadvertently helped me tell them, and who has supported me along my journey, whether we talk all the time or haven't heard a word from each other in years, whether alive or passed on to the next adventure: thank you for making your indelible mark in my life. I can't imagine my story without you in it. Thank you especially to Maryum Ali Campbell, Katie Allen, Ben Brody, Heather Boychuk, Alison Campanello, Hannah Currier, Nicole Dallochio, Brian Henretta, Christina Powers, Sarah and Alberto Principe, Jen Ramirez, Nina Ramon, Kate Ramsey, Suzanne Ringle, Jessika and Justin Savage, Lilliane Waelder, Megan Williams ... and to one of my favorite former staff sergeants who shall not be named, out of deep respect for his privacy and his invaluable advice to "Trust no one" at the very beginning of my short-lived military career.

... every reader of my "online diary," who became some of my dearest real-life friends—in memory of Rayna, Michael, Barb, Poola the Pirate, and the inimitable Turquoise Taylor Grant.

... all of the authors, artists, performers, and activists who've validated the truth I witnessed and opened my eyes to the pervasiveness of the military-industrial complex: thank you for showing me how to constantly keep learning and asking questions, to stay humble and open to new perspectives, and to share what I learn without being held back by fear. Thank you to my fellow anti-war veterans, including members of Iraq Veterans Against the War, Veterans For Peace, Vietnam Veterans Against the War, and all our civilian allies and accomplices, for your friendship, mentorship, leadership, inspiration, education, and all forms of support through the years (even if we've fallen out of touch or favor with each other), especially: Farah M., Steve Acheson, Jan Barry, Chantelle Bateman, Clare Bayard, Kyle Bibby, Lovella Calica, Joe Callan, Drew Cameron, Lee Camp, Adele Carpenter, Brittney Chantele, Diedra Cobb, Claude Copeland, Paul Cox, Crystal Cravens, Bill Creighton, Monique D'hoohge, Alice Deanin, Rosa del Duca, Penny Dex, Latonia Dixon, Kelly Dougherty, Robin Eckstein, Eddie Falcon, Alex Ferencz, Shawna Foster, Rush Frazier, Stephen Funk, Eleanor Goldfield, Zollie Goodman, Nicole Goodwin, Amos Gregory, Robin Guthrie, Dottie Guy, Ryan Harvey, Matt Hoh, Aaron Hughes, Lori Hurlebaus, Jenna and Ryan Johnson, Antonia Juhasz, Sonia Kennebeck, Scott Kimball, Poppy Kohnerova, Sarah Lazare, Nate Lewis, Heather Linebaugh, Lisa Ling, Robin Long, Talia Lugacy, Siri Margerin, Mike Marion, Maggie Martin, Jason Matherne, Drew Matott, Melanie McConathy, Michael McPhearson, Jason Moon, Nick Morgan, Robynn Murray, Hal Muskat, Aaron Myracle, Vrnda and Ronald Noel, Sara Nolte, Katherine Nguyen, Scott

Olsen, Jenny Pacanowski, Bill Perry, Cassidy Regan, Ward Reilly, Garett Reppenhagen, Amy Rising, Paula Rogovin, Amber Rose, Jen Rogue, Stephanie Rugoff, Ann Hirschman Schremp, Joshua Shepherd, Sonia Silbert, Danny Sjursen, Amanda Spitfire, Pallas Stanford, Matt Stys, Karla Terry, Miles E. Thomas, Ehren Tool, Jessica Troy, Krystal Two Bulls, Regina Vasquez, Robert Vessels, Hart Viges, Joyce Wagner, Sabrina Waller, Jason Washburn, Ash-Lee Woodard Henderson, Ann Wright, Eli Wright, Betty Yu, Amber Zora ... and in memory of Evan Bogart, June Brumer, and dear departed comrades Jacob George, Ethan DeFiant Kreutzer, and Drake Logan, whose fire still fuels my passion for speaking out against the system that stole their will to stay in this life.

... my peers and professors at UC Berkeley, where I took my first deep dive into the complexities of U.S. involvement in the Middle East: thank you for helping me understand the realities I could only observe as a soldier, and for deepening my appreciation for the people, cultures, and history of a region I'd previously only briefly occupied as an outside invader. Thank you especially to Hatem Bazian and his Islamophobia Research and Documentation Project, which allowed me to make a personal exploration into the origins of anti-Arab policies and sentiments within the U.S., and to Kiren Chaudhry, Emily Drumsta, Munis Faruqui, John Hayes, Minoo Moallem, Mahmood Monshipourri, Rhea Myerscough, Genevieve Negrón-Gonzales, and Leilt Seblega of the Berkeley City College TAP program, for your contributions to my education on the nature and impact of U.S. imperialism around the world and at home, and for your patience with me as I learned.

... all who have been part of my writing, editing, and publishing process: the hours you've spent with these stories have been invaluable, and your reflections have helped this book grow into itself. I'm grateful for my professors, cohort, and community at

Naropa University and the Jack Kerouac School of Disembodied Poetics, whose guidance and insights helped me shape this project into its final form, and for all the other dear writers and readers who've taken time with these pages. Thanks especially to my dear partner-in-podcast Sarah Baranauskas, and to Anastasia Brennan, Chris Chady, J'Lyn Chapman, Serena Chopra, Sam Cook, Drew Dean, Corinne Dekkers, Natalie Earnhart, Debby Englander, Eleanor Goldfield, Emma Gomis, Samantha Hart, Stephanie Michele Hempel, Kathy Jacobsen, Eric Mayer, Sammy Moore, Jaime Morton, Margaret Randall, Kendra Richard, Sarah Riggs, Maxfield Sparrow, Swanee, Chloe Tsolakoglou, Jeffrey Pethybridge, Julie van Amerongen, and Anne Waldman. One of the earliest readers (and instigators) of my first full draft, Mark Chapman, is no longer with us, but he was a dear and important friend and supporter of my life and work while he was here. He always encouraged and helped me to be a better version of myself, and I feel fortunate to have had the chance to thank him for that in person.

... Brooke MacNamara, Lisa Gibson, and the sangha you have so lovingly gathered: thank you for helping me stay sane while writing this book and living this life.

... all of the musicians who have inspired and influenced me to turn my opinions into songs as well as stories—thank you especially to Barbara Dane, Kimya Dawson, Ed Hamell, Talia Keys, Country Joe McDonald, Nathan Moore, and Mary Prankster—for your music, your words, and for reaching back when I reached out.

An extra special round of gratitude goes to everyone who pledged the Kickstarter campaign for this book, giving me the final financial boost I needed for production and promotion costs: Jim Anderson, Allen Axelband, Katie B., Sarah Baranauskas, Chris Bartle, Valerie Blaha, Randy Brown, Gina Bua, Paul Buckley,

Cesar C, Chris Chady, Erica Cole, Crystal Colon, Ann-Marie Cowsill, Keith Dawson, Drew Dean, Alice Deanin, Rosa del Duca and Nicholas Leither, Penny Dex and David Hasenjaeger, Heather Estey, Lisa Ezra, Rachel Friedman and N.A. Poe, Tami G, Steven Gardiner, Elizabeth Gene, Joanna Giuttari, Jon Goodman, Sakina Abdul Haqq, Patty Hartley, Linda and Chris Hauser, Allegra Heidelinde, Timothy Heider, Christopher Hopkins, Michelle Horton, Lori Hurlebaus, Joanna Johansen, Jeff Koelemay, Ariana Kramer, Kristen, Elesha Lopez, Jason Mack, Eric Mayer, Kimberly McCreary, Rachel McNeill, Michael T. McPhearson, Kat Meadows, David Mengel, Celeste Di Iorio Morin and Cary Morin, Suzy Mound, Hal Muskat, Vrnda and Ronald Noel, Jenny Pacanowski, Elizabeth Papa, Phil Pflager, Jen Ramirez, Ythsta Resovich, Dennis Ross, Michael Roth, Stephanie Rugoff, Sabrina, Hope Savage, Susan Schacher, Ann Hirschman Schremp, Jessika and Justin Savage, Brenna Schaetzle, Janet Siler, Ana Sosa, Larry Swearingin, TMFK and Melahn Atkinson, Rob V., Lilliane Waelder, Kairo Weber, Evan Weissman, Brian Woodbury, Basia and Stephen Yakaitis, Susan and Jim Yobp, and John Zutz.